'Tender, honest, angry, loyal, thi
balances the life, illness and death of
the feelings of his independent son . .
affecting passages of the book, Blak
and even murderous feelings in the face of grief and
mortality. At his saddest he asks what consolation art can
be. With writing as beautiful as his, he answers the
question.' – *The Times*

'A masterpiece of devotion, wit and poetic grace.'
– *Mail on Sunday*

'A splendid book . . . it leaps with life.' – *Irish Times*

'Morrison's humanity shines through this marvellous
memoir.' – *New Statesman & Society*

'An extraordinary, moving account of a son's relationship
with his father.' – *Marie Claire*

'Blake Morrison has written a moving tribute for the living
as much as the dead in compelling prose, untinted by
sentiment.' – *Time Out*

'A fine and courageous book.' – *Sunday Independent*

And when did you last see your father?

Blake Morrison was born in Skipton, Yorkshire. He is the author of two collections of poetry, *Dark Glasses* and *The Ballad of the Yorkshire Ripper*; of a children's book, *The Yellow House*; of critical studies of the Movement and Seamus Heaney; and is co-editor of *The Penguin Book of Contemporary British Poetry. And when did you last see your father?* won the Waterstone's/Volvo/Esquire Award for Non-Fiction and the J.R. Ackerley Prize for Autobiography in 1993. His latest book is the highly acclaimed *As If*.

BLAKE MORRISON

And when did you last see your father?

Granta Books

London

Granta Publications, 2/3 Hanover Yard, London N1 8BE

First published in Great Britain by Granta Books 1993
This edition published by Granta Books 1998

A CIP catalogue record for this book is available
from the British Library.

3 5 7 9 10 8 6 4 2

Printed and bound in Great Britain
by Mackays of Chatham PLC

Contents

In the morning, when everything was done, I gave her a long last farewell kiss in her coffin. I bent over her, and as I lowered my head into the coffin I felt the lead buckle under my hands . . . The grave was too narrow, the coffin wouldn't fit. They shook it, pulled it, turned it this way and that; they took a spade and crowbars, and finally a gravedigger trod on it—just above Caroline's head—to force it down. I was standing at the side, holding my hat in my hand; I threw it down with a cry.

. . . I wanted to tell you all this, thinking it would give you pleasure. You are sufficiently intelligent, and love me enough, to understand that word 'pleasure', which would make the bourgeois laugh.

Flaubert, letter to Maxime DuCamp, March 1846

. . . The odds is gone,
And there is nothing left remarkable
Beneath the visiting moon.

Antony and Cleopatra

Oulton Park

A HOT SEPTEMBER Saturday in 1959, and we are stationary in Cheshire. Ahead of us, a queue of cars stretches out of sight around the corner. We haven't moved for ten minutes. Everyone has turned his engine off, and now my father does so too. In the sudden silence we can hear the distant whinge of what must be the first race of the afternoon, a ten-lap event for saloon cars. It is quarter past one. In an hour the drivers will be warming up for the main event, the Gold Cup—Graham Hill, Jack Brabham, Roy Salvadori, Stirling Moss and Joakim Bonnier. My father has always loved fast cars, and motor-racing has a strong British following just now, which is why we are stuck here in this country lane with hundreds of other cars.

My father does not like waiting in queues. He is used to patients waiting in queues to see him, but he is not used to waiting in queues himself. A queue, to him, means a man being denied the right to be where he wants to be at a time of his own choosing, which is at the front, now. Ten minutes have passed. What is happening up ahead? What fathead has caused this snarl-up? Why are no cars coming the other way? Has there been an accident? Why are there no police to sort it out? Every two minutes or so my father gets out of the car, crosses to the opposite verge and tries to see if there is movement up ahead. There isn't. He gets back in and steams some more. The roof of our Alvis is down, the sun beating on to the leather upholstery, the chrome, the picnic basket. The hood is folded and pleated into the mysterious crevice between the boot and the narrow back seat where my sister and I are scrunched together as usual. The roof is nearly always down, whatever the weather: my father loves fresh air, and every car he has owned has been a convertible, so that he can have fresh air. But the air today is not fresh. There is a pall of high-rev exhaust, dust, petrol, boiling-over engines.

In the cars ahead and behind, people are laughing, eating sandwiches, drinking from beer bottles, enjoying the weather, settling into the familiar indignity of waiting-to-get-to-the-front. But my father is not like them. There are only two things on his mind: the invisible head of the queue and, not unrelated, the other half of the country lane, tantalizingly empty.

'Just relax, Arthur,' my mother says. 'You're in and out of the car like a blue-tailed fly.'

But being told to relax only incenses him. 'What can it be?' he demands. 'Maybe there's been an accident. Maybe they're waiting for an ambulance.' We all know where this last speculation is leading, even before he says it. 'Maybe they need a doctor.'

'No, Arthur,' says my mother, as he opens the door again and stands on the wheel-arch to crane ahead.

'It must be an accident,' he announces. 'I think I should drive up and see.'

'No, Arthur. It's just the numbers waiting to get in. And surely there must be doctors on the circuit.'

It is one-thirty and silent now. The saloon race has finished. It is still over an hour until the Gold Cup itself, but there's another race first, and the cars in the paddock to see, and besides . . .

'Well, I'm not going to bloody well wait here any longer,' he says. 'We'll never get in. We might as well turn round and give up.' He sits there for another twenty seconds, then leans forward, opens the glove compartment and pulls out a stethoscope, which he hooks over the mirror on the windscreen. It hangs there like a skeleton, the membrane at the top, the metal and rubber leads dangling bow-legged, the two ivory earpieces clopping bonily against each other. He starts the engine, releases the handbrake, reverses two feet, then pulls out into the opposite side of the road.

'No,' says my mother again, half-heartedly. It could be that he is about to do a three-point turn and go back. No it couldn't . . .

My father does not drive particularly quickly past the marooned cars ahead. No more than twenty miles an hour. Even so, it *feels* fast, and arrogant, and all the occupants turn and stare as they see us coming. Some appear to be angry. Some are shouting. 'Point to the stethoscope, pet,' he tells my mother, but she has slid down sideways in her passenger seat, out of sight, her bottom resting on the floor, from where she berates him.

'God Almighty, Arthur, why do you have to do this? Why can't you wait like everyone else? What if we meet something coming the other way?' Now my sister and I do the same, hide ourselves below the seat. Our father is on his own. He is not with us, this bullying, shaming undemocratic cheat. Or rather, we are not with him.

My face pressed to the sweet-smelling upholstery, I imagine what is happening ahead. I can't tell how far we have gone, how many blind corners we have taken. If we meet something, on this narrow country lane, we will have to

11

reverse past all the cars we have just overtaken. That's if we can stop in time. I wait for the squeal of brakes, the clash of metal.

After an eternity of—what?—two minutes, my mother sticks her head up and says, 'Now you've had it,' and my father replies, 'No, there's another gate beyond,' and my sister and I raise ourselves to look. We are up level with the cars at the head of the queue, which are waiting to turn left into the brown ticket holders' entrance, the plebs' entrance. A steward steps out of the gateway towards us, but my father, pretending not to see him, doesn't stop. He drives ahead, on to a clear piece of road where, two hundred yards away, half a dozen cars from the opposite direction are waiting to turn into another gateway. Unlike those we have left behind, these cars appear to be moving. Magnanimous, my father waits until the last of them has turned in, then drives through the stone gateposts and over the bumpy grass to where an armbanded steward in a tweed jacket is waiting by the roped entrance.

'Good afternoon, sir. Red ticket holder?' The question does not come as a shock: we have all seen the signs, numerous and clamorous, saying RED TICKET HOLDERS' ENTRANCE. But my father is undeterred.

'These, you mean,' he says, and hands over his brown tickets.

'No, sir, I'm afraid these are brown tickets.'

'But there must be some mistake. I applied for red tickets. To be honest, I didn't even look.'

'I'm sorry, sir, but these are brown tickets, and brown's the next entrance, two hundred yards along. If you just swing round here, and . . . '

'I'm happy to pay the difference.'

'No, you see the rules say . . . '

'I know where the brown entrance is, I've just spent the last hour queueing for it by mistake. I drove up here because I thought I was red. I can't go back there now. The queue stretches for miles. And these children, you know, who'd been looking forward . . . '

By now half a dozen cars have gathered behind us. One of them parps. The steward is wavering.

'You say you applied for red.'

'Not only applied for, paid for. I'm a doctor, you see'—he points at the stethoscope—'and I like being near the grand-stand.'

This double *non-sequitur* seems to clinch it.

'All right, sir, but next time please check the tickets. Ahead and to your right.'

This is the way it was with my father. Minor duplicities. Little fiddles. Money-saving, time-saving, privilege-attaining fragments of opportunism. The queue-jump, the backhander, the deal under the table. Parking where you shouldn't, drinking after hours, accepting the poached pheasant and the goods off the back of a lorry. 'They' were killjoys, after all—'they' meaning the establishment to which, despite being a middle-class professional, a GP, he didn't belong; our job, as ordinary folk trying to get the most out of life, was to outwit them. Serious lawbreaking would have scared him, though he envied and often praised to us those who had pulled off ingenious crimes, like the Great Train Robbers or, before them, the men who intercepted a lorry carrying a large number of old bank-notes to the incinerator ('Still in currency, you see, but not new so there was no record of the numbers and they couldn't be traced. Nobody got hurt, either. Brilliant, quite brilliant'). He was not himself up to being criminal in a big way, but he was lost if he couldn't cheat in a small way: so much of his pleasure derived from it. I grew up thinking it absolutely normal, that most Englishmen were like this. I still suspect that's the case.

My childhood was a web of little scams and triumphs. The time we stayed at a hotel situated near the fifth tee of a famous golf-course—Troon, was it?—and discovered that if we started at the fifth hole and finished at the fourth we could avoid the clubhouse and green fees. The private tennis clubs and yacht clubs and drinking clubs we got into (especially on Sundays in dry counties of Wales) by giving someone else's name: by the time the man on the door had failed to find it, my father would have read the names on the list upside-down—'There, see, Wilson—no Wilson, I said, not Watson'; if all else failed, you could try slipping the chap a one-pound note. With his innocence, confidence and hail-fellow cheeriness, my father could usually talk his way into anything, and usually, when caught, out of anything.

He failed only once. We were on holiday, skiing, in Aviemore, and he treated us to a drink in one of the posher hotels. On his way back from the lavatories, he noticed a sauna room for residents near a small back entrance. For the rest of the week, we sneaked in to enjoy residents' saunas. On the last day, though, we were towelling ourselves dry when an angry manager walked in: 'You're not residents, are you?'

I waited for some artless reply—'You mean the saunas aren't open to the public, like the bars? I thought . . . '—but for once my father stammered and looked guilty. We ended up paying some exorbitant sum *and* being banned from the hotel. I was indignant. I discovered he was fallible. I felt conned.

Oulton Park, half an hour later. We have met up with our cousins in the brown car park—they of course got here on time—and brought them back to the entrance to the paddock. My father has assumed that, with the red tickets he's wangled, we are entitled to enter the paddock for nothing, along with our guests. He is wrong. Tickets to the paddock cost a guinea. There are ten of us. We're talking serious money.

'We'll buy *one*, anyway,' my father is saying to the man in the ticket-booth, and he comes back with it, a small brown paper card, like a library ticket, with a piece of string attached to a hole at the top so you can thread it through your lapel. 'Let me just investigate,' he says, and disappears through the gate, the steward seeing the lapel-ticket and nodding him through: no stamp on the hand or name-check. In ten minutes or so my father is back. He whispers to my Uncle Ron, hands him the ticket and leads the rest of us to a wooden-slatted fence in a quiet corner of the car park. Soon Uncle Ron appears on the other side of the fence, in an equally quiet corner of the paddock, and passes the ticket through the slats. Cousin Richard takes the ticket this time and repeats the procedure. One by one we all troop round: Kela, Auntie Mary, Edward, Jane, Gillian, my mother, me. In five minutes, all ten of us are inside.

'Marvellous,' my father says. 'Three pounds eleven shillings and we've got four red tickets and ten of us in the paddock. That'd be costing anyone else twenty guineas. Not bad.'

We stand round Jack Brabham's Cooper, its bonnet opened like a body on an operating table, a mass of tubes and wires and gleamy bits of white and silver. I touch the metal behind the cockpit and think of my green Dinky car, no. 8, which I call Jack Brabham in the races I have on the carpet against the red Ferrari no. 1 (Fangio) and the silver Maserati no. 3 (Salvadori) and the yellow Jaguar no. 4 (Stirling Moss). I like Jack Brabham to win, and somehow he always does, though I swear I push the cars equally. It is quiet at home, pretending. Here at Oulton Park it's not quiet: there's a headachy mix of petrol and sun and engine roar.

Later, Moss overtakes Brabham on lap six, and stays there

for the next sixty-nine laps. A car comes off the circuit between Lodge Corner and Deer Leap, just along from where we're standing. There is blood, splintered wood and broken glass. My father disappears—'just to see if I can help.' He comes back strangely quiet, and whispers to my mother: 'Nothing I could do.'

Airedale

HE IS SITTING on the far side of the bed, or someone is, someone in a thin green gown, not at all like him. Hospitals have a way of disorienting people. But it can't be this. My father is used to hospitals. This hospital, Airedale, is the one to which, in his last decade as a GP, he would refer most of his cases. This ward, Ward 19, is one to which he's come, even since retirement, to see old patients. Even this room, no. 2, a private room given to him because he is, or was, a doctor, he knows from earlier visits. But today he isn't visiting. Today he's the patient. Today the visitor is me.

If it it were my father visiting, this person on the far side of the bed would get short shrift. *What do you call this, then? A nightie? Not quite your style, is it? Where are your flannel pyjamas?* He has a white cotton blanket over his knees: *What, in this hot room, a baby blanket? Let's have those windows open, let's get some air in the place.* He turns his head only a fraction when I enter: *Come on, cheer up, it might never happen.* But it will happen, he knows it will happen, we all know it will happen, sooner rather than later, and that is why I'm here.

'Feeling rough, Dad?' I ask.

'Too true.'

I hug him a moment, then slide two chairs beside the bed: a small plastic chair next to his, for me; and a slightly more comfortable armchair—actually, as minimal as that, a chair with arms—for my mother.

Close up, I see how loose the skin is hanging on his face. He isn't pale—the old tanned ruddiness is there—but his Bournville-dark eyes have lost their light: no one now could mistake him, as he sometimes used to be mistaken, for Micky Rooney. His neck seems stiff; his head is thrust slightly forward, like a tortoise's from its shell: it is as if it is being pushed from the back to offset the recession at the front, the literal loss of face. His hands, when he takes a sip from the clear plastic beaker of water, are gently shaking. He seems to be on the other side of some invisible divide, a screen of pain.

'You're feeling better than yesterday, though?'

'Yes.'

'And it is only four days since the operation.'

'True.'

'And Mum says the doctors are pleased.'

'If I could just sort my waterworks out. My tummy's so swollen.'

'Tummy': a word he's always used, even to adults, part of the old-fashioned bedside manner, an on-the-level-with-children cosiness. I can see him peering down at me, pouched eyes and churred Whitbread breath, in the long night of some childhood temperature, the walls coming and going, and him the only fixed point: 'Is your tum-tum hurting? Tell Daddy where it hurts.' Tum-ti-tum-tum-tum: there's a music of trust here—no need to panic about illness or ring for the doctor or rush to the chemists, because my parents *are* doctors, their surgery is our home, and the chemist is on our bathroom shelves. But now it's me leaning over him. Now I'm being the parent, the doctor, the one with the bedside manner.

'Does it hurt peeing?'

'Not much. I had a catheter in yesterday, but I was peeing round it, so they took it out. Last night I wet the bed.'

'But it's uncomfortable?'

'My penis is so engorged: it's like elephantiasis, I tell you.'

After 'tummy', the textbook chill of 'penis' seems odd. Perhaps it's in deference to my mother: a little later, when she's out of the room, he shouts from the lavatory, over the faint squits and squishes, 'There's more piss coming out of my arse than my prick.' But 'penis' sounds correct, denoting something distant from him, a part that's barely part of him any more. There's no wry nod and wink, no after-leer, with the reference to engorgement. If anything tells me he's ill, it's this neglect of the opportunity for a dirty laugh.

'Soup, doctor?' asks the student nurse from the door— Kieran, it says, on his lapel. 'Oh, no,' he says, consulting his clipboard, 'You're down for orange juice.'

'Did I ask for orange juice?'

'It says so. But you can have soup.'

'What soup is it?'

'Vegetable.'

'I'll have the soup.'

Kieran reappears with a white porcelain soup-bowl sloshing over the plastic tray and paper napkin, and puts it down on the wheely table. My father holds a trembling spoon and sucks at it, the liquid only, not the little vegetables floating around, which he avoids as if they were the equivalent size and hardness of a chop.

My mother and I, sitting there, silently will him to eat more, more. Then Kieran is back. 'How are we getting on, then?' he asks in a slow, loud, deliberate voice. I want to scream at him: 'This is my father, you dickhead. He's not some decrepit invalid to be patronized.' But of course that is exactly what he is.

Kieran gathers the soup things.

'And hotpot to follow?'

'I can't have ordered hotpot,' says my father. It is his favourite dish, after tripe and onions. Once a week at least, throughout my childhood, my mother would cook it in a big, brown earthenware pot: onions, scrag end, butter, salt and pepper—best of all the crispy-brown potatoes at the top.

'Surely I said fish.'

'I'll check, doctor.'

Kieran returns, plate in hand. 'It's chicken hotpot.'

'Ah, chicken.'

But it might as well be stone. My father chews away for a minute or two, then spits it out. There are two little mounds of mashed potatoes, too, but he ignores these completely.

'It tastes like paraffin,' he says, not whingeing, merely reporting. 'And it's so dry. It's like swallowing sawdust, or twigs.'

He lays his fork down, and his head back on the pillow, his features blurry. I think of a Francis Bacon painting, a reclining figure, discomposed, decomposed. I think of a phrase from Auden: *We seldom see a sarcoma/As far advanced as this*. And then I think how indecent it is to think of such things, for my mind to wander off and leave him now, here, at such a time.

Exhausted, he raises a cup of cold tea to his lips, then sets it down shakily in its saucer. It is six o'clock and he is ready for his night's sleep.

Three months before, my parents had come south for someone's eightieth birthday party, the sort of jaunt they liked: getting up at dawn, driving a hundred miles before breakfast, the open road, under their own steam, not stopping off for meals or staying with anyone but cooking and sleeping in their Bedford Dormobile (later traded up for a German Hymobile), restless septuagenarians free to come and go as they pleased, a proud-to-be-pensioners sticker on the rear window—GET EVEN: LIVE LONG ENOUGH TO BE A PROBLEM TO YOUR CHILDREN. But this particular outing had gone wrong. In the evening they stopped for a meal at a pub. My mother needed to use the telephone and set out for the bright cubist box a hundred yards away, not knowing that between her and it there was a low wall and, beyond, a four-foot drop. Puzzled when she didn't return, my father went out to look, first on foot, then in his Hymo. The headlights picked up a bundle of clothes on the concrete below the ha-ha, a bloodied heap. He thought she might have broken her neck, and dared not move her. At Stoke Mandeville hospital, the X-rays found two small breaks in the vertebrae and hand, and there was heavy bruising to the face, neck, arms, legs.

'She's going to be all right, but we won't be coming on to see you,' he said when he rang next morning, making it sound like a nursery tumble rather than a case for the country's leading spinal injuries hospital. I drove up the day after, his Hymobile conspicuous in the car park. My mother was sitting up, cuts, a black eye, a bright blue bruise on her forehead, but healthily peeved that owing to lack of space they had put her in a men's ward. My father ushered me away as soon as he decently could, out to the car park and the *Financial Times*. He wanted to talk about his investments. He wanted to talk about my tax returns. He did not want to talk about the accident—though later he admitted that he'd gone back to take photographs of where the fall happened, the blood on the pavement, 'in case we decide to sue the pub.'

Four days later he drove her back to Yorkshire, having talked the hospital into an early discharge—wasn't he a doctor, and wouldn't she be better off at home than on a ward, and didn't he have a Hymobile, with a bed she could lie flat on, kitted out as well as any ambulance? She was up and walking within a fortnight.

So when my father began complaining of stomach pains and loss of appetite, we took it to be delayed shock—the penalty of denial, nothing more.

'The pain, Dad: that's where they cut into you?'

'Yes.'

'And it's still very sore?'

'Too true.'

'Is the pain on the inside, or is it the scar on the surface?'

'Both.'

'You had a blood transfusion yesterday?'

'Yes.'

'So you must have lost a lot of blood.'

'No, it was routine, Dr Taggart says.'

Every lunchtime, eating sandwiches on high stools by the kitchen Aga, or maybe shepherd's pie at the dining-room table, my mother and father would discuss their caseloads: who had mysterious pains in the arms, who had been vomiting for three days; who had gone into hospital, who had come out; who— my sister and I used to giggle at the word—was 'fibrillating'. Then the phone would ring and he'd be probing the unfortunate caller: how long had she been complaining of this? where was the pain exactly? did she have a temperature, catarrh, diarrhoea? It was the same whenever I was ill, or, later, when my children were, or when someone on holiday began bombarding him with ailments, as they invariably did when they discovered he was a doctor. I'm used to these medical cross-examinations (sometimes, with hypochondriacs and time-wasters, very cross indeed), the relentless questions, the answers to which might mean him going out in the middle of the night. But I'm not used to my father being on the receiving end.

'Is it a long scar where they opened you up?'

'Look.'

He tries to show me, but pulling up his nightshirt is a laborious task. He puffs and tugs at the hem. When he gets there I see the white fluffy dressing running from just below his chest down to his pubic hair—or where his pubic hair should have been.

'They shaved you.'

'Yes.'

'The legs as well?'

'No, not the legs.'

I have not seen his legs until now, because of the baby blanket. The ankles rise out of his felt moccasin slippers like loaves, twice their usual size. The shin bones are red and shiny. The hairs *are* there, I can see that now, but under the blotchy sheen they have lost their spiky darkness. When he rises moon-slow to walk to the bathroom, I see how swollen his legs really are. They were always so slender and shapely, a woman's legs, you might say (though men's legs are often like this—in drag, the bit from the waist down, the nylons and high heels, is the most convincing). Perhaps my father's legs seemed especially graceful because they fitted so oddly with the rest of him—the flabby waist, the vast ribcage, the blunt head. He seemed, sometimes, like a random assemblage from that children's card game, Misfits, where you draw the gazelle's legs, the elephant's torso and the head of a seal. On the beach in summer, standing by the water's edge in his shorts, he resembled a wading bird—the impossibly thin pins, the huge puffed chest. Now his legs are bloated, as if everything he drank sloshed straight down to his ankles. Out of breath, he reaches the bathroom door and gently closes it behind him.

It was on Hallowe'en that I knew something was wrong. He had come down three months before to give me 'advice' about buying a house—i.e. to decide where I should live. I took him through the shortlist and when he saw the house I'd anticipated would be his choice (a big, bland three-storey affair from the fifties, set in a wide road that seemed more John Cheever country than south-east London), he told me to go for it, that he'd chip in the extra money, that this was a great place for three kids to grow up in, and sod my reservations. He wanted to meet the owner, to see if he could beat down the price some more. He wanted to take photographs of the stairs and landing to discuss with his own builder, up in Yorkshire, the feasibility of a loft extension. He wanted the architect's plans. He wanted the name of every estate agent in the area so he could visit them and check I hadn't missed something better. He talked about helping me decorate the place, and I knew I'd cave in and move there, never admitting how large a part of me hated the house, let alone how wrong it felt, at forty, to be financially and in other ways so dependent on him. That night I made an offer on the house and we got drunk together. Next day he was off again.

In October, completion approaching, I readied myself for the arguments we'd have when he discovered that I'd hired a removal firm. 'But why? I've got the Hymobile, haven't I? I'm retired, I've got all the time in the world to help. Why spend good money when I could ferry all the furniture there for you?' I worried how I would break it to him that I didn't actually want him there for the move, that it would be better for him to come down a day or week or month or two later.

In the event the row didn't come—and nor did he. He didn't even propose coming. I put this down to his continuing anxiety about my mother's fall. I even wondered whether he was belatedly learning some tact. On Hallowe'en night the two removal vans pulled up outside the new house. A football team of carriers and packers filed in and out, bearing the first sofas and wardrobes as gingerly as if they were coffins, then, as the hours passed, beginning to sweat and swear and bump into each other, and still no end to the accumulated junk. A deeper darkness fell. Children at the open door asked 'Trick or treat?', and a painted lady in a witch's cloak introduced herself as a neighbour. Another witch asked if we had toffee for the spirit-children holding pumpkin skulls beside her. Finally the last packing case came off, and the men sat on the front step drinking lager. 'Look, a fox,' one of them said, and there it was, rooted to the lawn just a few yards away, a thief in the night, one of its front legs raised and tucked under, body tensed, nose lifted, sniffing the night air.

I rang my father next morning, from a gap in the scattered packing cases.

'Not this weekend, lad,' he replied to my invitation. 'I'm feeling a bit rough.'

'He's not himself,' my mother chipped in.

'Too true.'

His stomach pains worsened. I stopped asking him when he was coming. I even stopped describing how I'd been fixing bookshelves in the basement, knowing it would torment him to think of how he was missing out and how bad a job I was bound to be making. Then, a week after I'd moved, he rang me.

'They've fixed an investigatory op for next Thursday. They'd have done it tomorrow but for the warfarin I'm taking.'

'Warfarin?'

25

'Rat poison to you. To thin my blood and stop me having a coronary. Now the bloody stuff's so thin it won't clot. One advantage, though. It gives me time to come down before I go in. I thought you could do with some help on that house of yours.'

He arrived next evening. It was the last weekend he spent out of Yorkshire.

'Your mother has told you?'

'Yes.'

Dr Taggart looks like a cancer patient himself, strung out, fleshless, hollow-faced.

'Well, I don't know what more I can tell you. The last two patients I've had in his sort of condition, pain in the bowel, turned out to be infarcts, not cancer: that's what we'd hoped to find. Or if cancer, something we'd caught in good time. But I'm afraid when we opened him up we found the disease had spread too far.'

'It's inoperable, you're saying.'

'Yes. He is dying. We all die, sooner or later, but with him it will be sooner. It could have been his heart. He's been coming here with that for the past three years, and obviously there was a risk with the operation that it would give out. And it still might. But the probability is that cancer will be what kills him.'

'Will there be a lot more pain?'

'There shouldn't be, with this kind of cancer. Usually they just quietly fade away. Did your mother explain about the tube?'

'Sort of.'

'Basically we've bypassed the whole of his stomach, where the disease is, so that the bowel can function a bit better again, for a while. He's likely to suffer from diarrhoea, but that's preferable to the constipation he's had.'

That much was true. My father had recently described to me stopping at a Happy Eater on his way home from the last weekend at our house. 'I went to the gents and had to dig the shit out by hand, horrible, but there was no other way.'

'And you can't predict how long?'

'That's the one thing everyone wants to hear, and the one thing we can't tell them. There should be time for him to go home and sort his affairs out. I've known miraculous cases where people in his condition lasted a year.'

Friends had spoken to me consolingly of cancer patients who'd been told their number was up five years ago but were still going strong. Dr Taggart didn't seem to be saying that. He was talking of one year as a miracle. He was talking months— Easter, maybe even Christmas.

'Does attitude matter? He seems so defeated.'

'I've known people who just turn their faces to the wall and die. Fighting can give you more time. And I know he's a very active and positive man. The problem is, being so ill to start with, he may not feel like fighting.'

'You've told him?'

'He asked me the moment he came round. So I put him in the picture.'

'It's funny, he always said, if ever, he wouldn't want to know.'

'But when it came to it he did want to know. That doesn't mean he'll want to talk about it again. It's possible he'll deny it—people do, and there's nothing wrong with that. To say, *I've* not got cancer, not me, those doctors are fools or liars, is a kind of strength too.'

'And there's no treatment?'

'I don't see the point. Certainly not radiotherapy. I'll give him chemotherapy if he asks, but it can have some nasty side-effects. There is a vitamin course I might suggest to him—but being a doctor he may just say, Vitamins! Don't talk bloody nonsense.'

'He's always been keen on vitamins. I should put it to him.'

'I will.' Dr Taggart looks at his watch.

'Thanks for talking to me,' I say.

'Not at all.' He grips my hand. 'And I'm sorry.'

Back in Room 2, my father wants to hear what Dr Taggart said. He needs to know that I know, that I'm under no illusions. That's why he fixed for Dr Taggart to see me. Or perhaps it wasn't that at all. Perhaps he hopes I'll bring him something new, something different, something hopeful.

'He says he's very pleased with your progress. He says he expects you to go home next week.'

My father lifts a little at this. But soon he has sunk back on the pillows, turning in on whatever's eating away at him. I try to jolt him back by switching on the television. The news leads with two knifing incidents in London, a young constable stabbed to death, two other policemen in hospital.

'Bloody wogs, come over here and start killing people,' says my father. A *Daily Mail* and *Sunday Express* reader all his life, he has become noticeably more racist and reactionary over the last decade.

'Hang on, Dad, they didn't actually say . . . '

'Yes, but it's funny how often it's them, isn't it?'

I let it go, determined not to be provoked for once. The second item is about Gary Lineker's baby, eight weeks old and found to be suffering from a rare form of leukaemia. 'Terrible,' my father says, 'Terrible,' my mother agrees, and adds: 'You know who they've got along the ward here? That lad who's been a vegetable since Hillsborough. Life-support machine—everyone wants to turn it off, but the law won't allow it. Tragic.'

We all agree it's tragic, any child or young person dying or coming near to it—though two hours ago, on the train from Leeds, looking round the carriage full of people going home, a deadbeat young Friday crowd with glazed eyes and Walkmans, I'd have cheerfully swapped the life of anyone there for my father's.

It's seven-thirty, and my mother and I are saying good-night. It seems odd and cruel leaving him. But he doesn't want us there, will be happier thinking he's 'not a nuisance'. He hugs me longer than he usually would, then sits holding my mother's hand, the kind of tender, quiet thing he never does, something I want to feel touched by but which seems so untypical it's almost offensive: a late bloom, another man's flower. I've always imagined him dying in character—overtaking impatiently on too short a straight, or collapsing with a heart attack while rotavating an obstinate corner of the orchard. This new gentle-ness, his slow drained face above the bedsheets, seems a sort of death already.

We walk out into the dark, the cold, then drive up the long curve from the hospital's sodium glare, past the endless signs saying AIREDALE. I think how far I am and how far the meaning of the word AIREDALE is from when I first heard it at school. Then AIRE meant one of the rivers of the north, whose descending order my father helped me memorize as SUNWACD, pronounced sun-whacked—Swale, Ure, Nidd, Wharfe, Aire, Calder, Don. Then DALE meant the Yorkshire Dales, the hilly syllables of Borrowdale, Wensleydale, Ribblesdale, Malhamdale, the fells and streams we drove to on days out, and the lesser dale whose name I couldn't say right and never quite believed, Arkengarthdale. AIRE and DALE meant that drizzly past. But AIREDALE, the compound, means the unavoidable present—two blunt, hard, wiry syllables, not a soft limestone roll of the tongue. AIREDALE is the harsh, low-lit, single-storey sickness factory we're driving from into the night.

It's me at the wheel. My mother's driving, earlier, from the station where she collected me, had been alarming—she was using sidelights only, getting too close to things, going fast and slow in the wrong places. 'Bit knackered,' she says, tipping her head back. For years she has woken early, insomnia, waiting for the light, the milkman, the papers. And now she has something more to wake wide-eyed and worrying for, something even worse to get through—the trauma, the enervation of the ward, the harsh chemical glare. Juggernauts sweep past me on the A59, grit lorries and refrigerator trucks, and I think of her alone at the wheel, drifting off into their path, dead before him. When I turn to check she's belted in beside me, I find she's already fast asleep.

Tonsils

THE HOSPITAL BED is higher than mine: you have to climb
down, not step out. There's that horrid empty-stomach feeling,
like coming down from a wall or a ladder—the long gap before
your feet touch something solid, the middle-of-nowhere gulp
when you think you're going to fall. You have to backslide
down, pinning and arching your shoulders against the bedsheets
while you cast your legs out into space. And when your feet
touch the ground the floor is icy-cold marble, not warm and
ruggy like at home.

Beside the bed is a metal cupboard with a glass of water
on top. I don't like water. I want the blackcurrant juice in the
bottle behind it, which the nurse says I can't have. Beside the
water-glass, the bunch of flowers, the GET WELL cards, the
two oranges I'm also not allowed, there's a new present I
opened today, a model of Donald Campbell's Bluebird with a
working propeller. I wish there were a lake near home where
I could launch it. The only places I can think of are the dirty
river by the Armorides factory and the stream by the surgery
where I once saw boys paddling—but Bluebird needs flat
water, perfect water, at dawn. There is a boating pond at
Sough, but I have seen the wind on it, the lapping and foam.

My throat is sore still, though not as sore as yesterday or the day before. And tomorrow, the nurse says, I will be leaving—it has been a week, and that's the time most children stay here. I don't think the girl with the big head and the open mouth will be leaving. I think there's something more wrong with her than a week takes. Maybe that's why no one ever comes to see her even at the big visiting time in the evening. My mother and father have been every evening to see me, but it's a long drive. It would be better if there were hospitals where parents could sleep overnight. Once they brought my sister Gillian too, and once they came on their afternoon off—it was not really a visiting time, but Daddy said it was all right because he and Mummy are doctors.

When it stops being sore, will my throat feel different from before? It doesn't have as much inside now, without the tonsils. You don't need tonsils, my father says, in fact it's bad to have tonsils because they get sore and infected. Tonsils are two flaps of skin, a bit like tongues or folded birds' wings, beneath your Adam's apple. No one knows why they were put there, but now they are taking them out of children. The boy across from me had his out, and I don't think he looks any different, though I don't know what he looked like before. I've felt my neck with my fingers under the bedclothes, and it seems the same, on the outside anyway. But it still hurts drinking the water and eating the squelchy meat-and-potato pie and most of all swallowing the pills.

My father says, when it hurts, to think of the presents I've got—Bluebird, but also the Dinky BRM from Gillian and the *Eagle* annual from Granny. *Eagle* is my favourite comic—well, the only one I'm allowed. I've tried to work out if Dan Dare has tonsils, but you can't get a proper look at his neck because he mostly wears a helmet. The Mekon doesn't look as if he can have tonsils, his neck is so thin. He is supposed to be wicked but I like the way he rides round on a little tea-saucer or bubble and bosses everyone about. He has bags over his eyes, instead of under them like Daddy, and though he hates all earth-things his head is like a green globe. I showed Daddy the page where the Mekon destroys Treen civilization on Mercury by blowing them all up, and he said it looked like the H-bomb, the bomb the English and the other goodies dropped to end the war—my father was in the RAF, but a doctor not a pilot, and he was nowhere near that bomb.

They don't tell you what's for tea here until you get it, but it's usually jam sandwiches and a cup of tea (which is funny, giving cups of tea to children), and rice pudding or jelly. Then we can listen to the wireless or play with our toys, and then it's bedtime. They don't have a television here: I didn't expect they would, but I was hoping. We got ours last year, and my favourite programmes, apart from *Blue Peter* and *Double Your Money* and the one with Michael Miles when everyone shouts 'Open the Box,' is *Emergency Ward Ten*. On Fridays we're allowed to stay up till eight and watch it and drink lemonade. But the hospital on television isn't like this one because there aren't children and terrible things happen like car accidents.

Daddy says I have to eat to get well, even if it hurts. The nurse smiles at me when she brings the jam sandwiches. She smiles differently at the other nurses, and when she smiles at sister it is different again. I wish there were bubbles coming out of her head with words, like in *Eagle*. Thought bubbles would be a useful invention in real life.

When you wake in the night there are strange slapping and scraping noises on the marble, and sometimes screams, but I close my eyes, and pretend I'm at home, and think of my presents, and imagine the Mekon in his bubble, and I do not cry, Daddy, I do not, I do not.

Dogs

WE ENTER THE house through the garage, and the first thing I
see is the chestnut flash of Nikki, the dachshund, squirming at
us, his tail a frantic fox-brush sweeping the carpet. He hurls
himself towards my crotch, not making it, scrabbling at my
knee. As I bend to stroke him, he rolls over on his back, his
front paws flopping campily, double-jointedly, back on
themselves, his tail no longer a wide swishing metronome but
a stumpy, irregular thump on the floor. Warmth, fur, the
beating heart of a held creature: I'm resisting the soppiness of
this, or trying to. I push him away and think sternly of dog-
shit, of muzzles, of knotting, of a girlfriend scarred for life (a
neat crucifix on her left cheek) by the family terrier. But then
my hand goes searching along his jawline, and I'm a child
again, back in the doggy comforts of his father's house.

I look up and there are more dogs—a line of them in a
naff, pseudo-French drawing, legs crossed, faces agonized
under berets, waiting for their place at the lamppost; and a
photograph of Gunner and Terry, the golden labradors my
parents bought the year before I was born, their twelve pups
feeding out of a trough which my father must have cadged
from one of his farmers. Perhaps this was the same farmer high

up above Earby who, one snowbound winter, fell sick and could be visited only by helicopter—a helicopter which my father got to ride in by making friends, 'over a pint', with the pilot, who was inspecting pylons for the Yorkshire Electricity Board and who was persuaded to park his machine overnight on our back lawn ('safe as houses') rather than in the car park of his hotel over the way ('it'd get vandalized, you know'). After his doctor's flying visit, my father hit it off with farmers: word got round that, however isolated they were, he'd reach them; he had special privileges, perhaps even special powers; if your tractor toppled over on a farm-hand, he was the man to call. Only his labradors, with their tendency to chase sheep, jeopardized these relations.

Gunner and Terry lasted all my childhood, and after they died my father did without dogs for a while, in homage. Then he bought a long-haired dachshund, and that's what he's had ever since, sausage dog after sausage dog, most of them with the same name, Nikki. He felt awkward at first—a dachshund was such a small and effeminate dog to take out on a lead, especially for him with his big chest; a man's man with a woman's dog, he looked like something out of Laurel and Hardy. But as the years passed, despite my gentle mockery, he lost his self-consciousness and grew to depend on dachshunds. He even shared his beer with them, his nightly party trick: the nearly-empty pale ale bottle placed upright on the floor; the dog knocking the bottle over with its snout, and using a paw to tip the liquid into its mouth; the bottle dragged over to the edge of the rug and tipped again, a deeper tilt, for the dregs; a pint or two later, the sound of gnawing at the glass.

Of course, I prided myself on a fastidious distaste for all this cutesiness, this dogginess, and made a point of lecturing my father on the perils of dog-shit. In our regular disputes over the value of having a dog, I reckoned to win on the security question, pointing out as ungleefully as possible that Nikki had been in the house when it was burgled. But he always triumphed when it came to social usefulness: dogs help you meet people, he said, and proved it one summer when he made friends with a woman on the beach who, as well as owning a poodle, had a speedboat and water-skis to which we were given unlimited access. Dogs brought out the sentimentalist in him. He was still not properly over the death of his last Nikki; one Bonfire Night some years ago he had let the dog out by mistake, and the noise of fireworks drove it distractedly into the road. Or so he alleged: neighbours' reports that Nikki had crossed the road several times earlier that week to visit a bitch on heat down at the farm did nothing to allay his guilt and remorse. He found the corpse on the grass verge, and came home crying with it in his arms.

He has always cried easily: he cried when dogs and cats died; he cried when he left my sister at her boarding-school; he cried waving goodbye from under our chestnut tree the day I went off to university. So why had he taught me to be brave and hold it in? Why have I never been able to cry? Why can't I cry for him? Even now, shaking myself loose of the dog and at once coming across a photo of my father from a year ago—tanned, happy, arms round his grandchildren on the beach—even now the tears won't come.

I pour myself a large gin and tonic, then another. There are too many cracking-up photographs around, too many mementoes: even his shoes in the workshop, the neat shelves of them, left-right, left-right, the cold leather turning up at the toes. My mother and I sit by the fire with plates on our knees. We drink wine with the roast chicken, and she begins a litany of *if onlys*: if only my father had had himself checked out regularly; if only he'd not refused the barium meal they'd offered him a month ago; if only she'd not had her accident.

'But the doctor thinks the secondaries have been there two years,' I say.

'Yes, I know, but if only they'd caught it a bit earlier, he'd have been spared that month of terrible pain.'

'But he'd have known for that much longer,' I say, 'he'd have been devastated.'

'Yes . . . But if only he hadn't got so weak before the operation, maybe he'd have more fight.'

'But we don't want the agony drawn out.'

So we *yes*, *but* and *if only*, until, several drinks later, we both begin to drowse, brief lid-droops then deeper sleep. I wake to find myself staring into my sister's face on the sofa, a younger, browner, wrinklier face than mine (Gillian has inherited my father's fondness for sunbathing). Quiet, anxious, she sits with her hands tight in her lap as we talk. We don't see each other much now—only when I'm up or she's down. Our lives have been separate from the day she went off to boarding-school thirty years ago, after she failed her eleven-plus. She hated it there, in banishment, and after three years of unhappy letters finally wrote one of such misery that my father, opening it at surgery, walked out on his patients, drove straight up to the school in the Lake District and brought her home. But by then I was fifteen, and more than our sixteen-month difference in age seemed to separate us. It's only recently we've things in common again, the things we talk about now: houses, spouses, children.

At midnight I walk Gillian back to her house next door, past the outbuildings—barn, stables, pigsty, garage—of our old house, each of them now converted to a house or flat, a hamlet blazing where we had once played among hay or cobwebs. She clutches my arm. With her night-blindness—a rare eye condition—she sees poorly in bright sunlight, badly at dusk and not at all at night. At forty, she's already on to large-print books from the library.

'Are you all right?' I ask.

'Yes, if someone's holding me.'

'I meant about Dad. Are you coping?'

'I think so.'

We talk about the operation: she understands his condition only dimly as yet, knows it is cancer but not that it's terminal, is being let in on it gently, protected from its full glare. It's my father's usual way of doing things: Mum's a doctor, I'm a man, but Gill's the youngest, a woman and the sensitive one, and he wants her led there slowly. I'm not sure: her serenity alarms me; it's based on kindly lies, and I want to shock her with the truth; or if she knows more than she's letting on, I want us both to admit it. We reach her laundry room, back in the safe light, by the boiler, out of the cold, and I pause there, steeling myself to tell her more, to say at least, 'We're talking months, Gill, you know, not years.' But what comes out of me is 'Goodnight,' and a peck on the cheek, and then I walk back under the blank lit immensity to bed.

In our old house—The Rectory it had been, The Grange as my father renamed it—there'd been a billiard room, long and with tall windows, which my father filled with a full-size snooker table, bought at an auction in Otley. A lorry fetched it over, and we watched it being laboriously lifted out and reconstructed—the slates, the rubber cushions, the string pockets, the lawn of green felt, the scoreboard with the sliding arrow-marker. He played on the table every night for six months, taught me to play, too, even invited Freddie Trueman round for a game—a friend of our solicitor. A racy new life beckoned, smoke-filled and alcoholic (the room also contained an outsize drinks cupboard): I dreamt of a misspent adolescence, Yorkshire champion at thirteen, a precocious toff wizard of the felt. I discovered backspin, sidespin, how to stop the cue-ball dead; I potted colours from improbable angles—a wafer kiss of white on black, the erotic plock in the pocket. But one morning my father put a cloth over the table and kept it there forever after, disrobing it only for a week each Christmas.

The snooker table became his desk, its entire length covered with paper: invoices, receipts, newspaper clippings, share certificates, bank statements, you name it. Every night he would come back from the pub around eleven-thirty, pour himself a whisky, and sit—or rather stand—doing his 'paper-work' till one or one-thirty in the morning. I made a point of not getting involved. The paperwork was something to do with the investments left to him by his father, a mining engineer. It was hard work keeping on top of them, I knew that much: he never finished, and never left the table any tidier. When he retired and moved to the new house he built at the back of the old one, there was no room for a billiard table. His paperwork was now supposedly confined to a mere desk, though he quickly spread it across the study floor as well— splays of arithmetic and tax returns, a very large number of brown envelopes with mysterious headings.

Those envelopes, in a stack on the parental bed, are the first thing I see this morning. I have slept indecently well. My mother has not. When I go in with two mugs of tea, and take his place next to her (we are going to have to get used to that empty pillow), she's straight into her worries.

'I thought I'd better look at these. It's not the stocks and shares I fret about. I know about those. I used to call out the share prices to him from the newspaper, I've seen the portfolio. It's all the other stuff—these insurance policies and bonds and pensions and saving schemes. He's so many bits of paper, you wouldn't believe it. I just don't know what's in them.'

My mother's fear of the chaos she'll inherit is understandable, though I know she is really saying something else. She dreads the paperwork because paper will soon be all that remains of him. She can't cope with figures, because she can't cope with the figure we saw yesterday, the figure receding on that bed.

'This is his special file,' she says, reaching into her bedside table. 'Have a good look while I use the shower.'

It's the family tree he was drawing up, a task he took over from his Uncle Billy (whose oil-lush garage we used to stop at on days out to Southport), one which had him writing to relations wherever they could be traced. There doesn't seem to be much in the file—a few letters and postcards—but I'm not expecting revelations. Though my mother's Irish side is bogged in Celtic mist, on my father's the impression has always been clear: a family settling in Lancashire and living off the fat of the Industrial Revolution; stolid captains of industry and their little wives; red-brick detached houses within shouting distance (but there would never be any shouting in these homes) of Bolton or Manchester; unshowy northern affluence; an enthusiasm for cars, railways, practical and mechanical things. No poets, no artists; no divorces; a fair bit of drinking, but not so much as to give the family a bad name.

The frail elderly handwriting, the photos and memory fragments come as a shock: their version of family history is very different. Here's an impecunious start, Daniel Morrison writing to his son in 1868 to say he's 'middling well' and asking, 'being I'm out of work and tramping the last six weeks and on the road for England,' for money to be sent to 'your poor old father' c/o Dumfries Post Office. Later there's talk of steady jobs in mining or with ships' instruments or on the

Manchester Ship Canal. But in between, the record is of alcoholism and *Wanderlust* and early deaths through several generations: my father's cousin, four-year-old Neil, gored to death by a cow when he got too near its calf; Crawford, who fell from a pigeoncote at three, was confined thereafter to a spinal carriage, died at fourteen; Jessie, who at the same age got pregnant by a rich Jewish boy in Manchester, took to the streets to hide her shame from the family, was spotted begging with her sickly child bundle and brought home; Daniel's father, Alexander, who remarried after his first wife's early death, moved away and left his children to fend for themselves; another errant Daniel, who married the sister of his wife (who had died in childbirth) either in France or illegally, since British law did not then permit you to marry your wife's sister; Bunty, who lost her mother at six, her father the following year; and Robert, who was run over and killed by a horse-drawn beer dray, having that lunchtime more or less consumed the contents of one.

Telescoped, edited, misremembered, any family's past seems a catalogue of grief and dispersal. But so many early deaths, and between the lines the other stories of alcoholism and madness and miscarriage and venereal disease and haemorrhages and mining disasters . . . For my father to be facing death at seventy-five begins to seem, in such a family, not a tragedy of cut-shortness but a miracle of longevity. For him to have stuck it out with his children seems miraculous, too, when the heritage is of neglect—children put on trains with address labels round their necks or pleading with their fathers, 'at least come home for Christmas.' And where are all the doctors and businessmen I'd been led to think lay behind us? The talk here is of deck-chair attendants in Blackpool, idlers of the dance-hall or ice-rink, chancers joining the US Gold Rush. I'd have been cheered, once, to discover these departures from stolidity. But not today. It isn't just (just!) that my father is dying. Where he came from is dying too.

I pick up a photograph, a wonderful sepia set piece, the Blakemores *circa* 1895, my great-grandmother and her four children posed on a bench, two girls in lace dresses and frills, a besuited boy with a book open in his hand, and a baby in a bonnet. I look at them in their allotted roles—the Eternal Mother (she died within a year), the Proud Beauty (married a womanizer), the Scholar (gassed in the trenches), the Daddy's Girl (but Daddy remarried), the Baby of the Family (already with his bottle)—and I follow their stares back to the man taking the picture, the Absent Father, who had his story too, grief and nervous breakdown. I think how cruelly far the reality of their lives was from what the camera had chosen or predicted for them that day, and how the photo lost nothing in feeling for my knowing this, and how that must mean art can lie as much as it likes, or needs to, and we forgive it anything so long as it *is* art. The people captured here are real, and there's a *frisson* in knowing that, which you couldn't get from painting or fiction; but truth does not come into it at all.

I dress and wander into the kitchen, where Pat is, the 'maid' as we called her when she arrived in the mid-sixties as an eighteen-year-old, the 'housekeeper' as she has become since my parents retired, though 'live-in' might be closer to the mark (these days she studies at a local college and has her room in return for occasional cleaning), and 'companion' or 'nurse' are suddenly looming ahead. She sits on a stool eating toast and peanut butter, young-looking still under her dark hair, the temporary fill-in who has stayed a quarter of a century, whose home this now is. 'She's a great girl is Pat, she's like a daughter to us,' my father likes to say, who has, however, another daughter, real not surrogate, a son, too. It's some tribute to Pat, or some reflection of our odd upstairs-downstairs arrangements, that my sister and I have never felt usurped: she's no one's servant, but she's not quite family either, prefers to eat alone, knows when to withdraw, has decided which bits of the house are hers to feel free in—the kitchen, her bedroom—and which are not. Now the portable television she's watching beside the kitchen sink reports a stabbing in London, and she turns to give me a look—wry, stoic, bereft—that tells me she knows how ill my father is, and that his death when it comes will be as hard for her, who shares his house and loves him, as for me, his far-away son.

I make us tea, she makes us more tea, then I walk down the garden. Over the wall, to the right, is the old house. My father had bought it from the Church of England for 2,500 pounds in 1954, and then spent another 5,000 pounds doing it up, an expense he always resented (if the practice hadn't been so busy, he'd have done all the work himself, not just mucked in at weekends), but which he made up for thirty years later when he retired and almost single-handedly built a new house in its grounds. The site was the paddock where I used to play solitary games of football—once my field of dreams, now his. Here, outside his dining-room, is where one of my goals used to be; there, down by his rockery, was the other. The trees that ran along one side of the pitch are still here, though lopped to let light in, and the wind is blowing through them as it used to when I was Ray Pointer and Jimmy McIlroy and the rest of the Burnley team. I was all the opposition players, too, and tried to stick one past myself between the metal posts hung with my father's strawberry nets. It was here I'd come after the final whistle of the 1962 Cup Final, to put right the scoreline: Tottenham Hotspur 3, Burnley 1, the television had said, but that wasn't how it ended on my pitch. The trees were ecstatic supporters then. Later I lay on my back beneath the trees, and heard the wind in them like a stream, and pretended I was listening to the sadness of passing time, and I knew one day I'd come back and the sadness would be real. Now I am here.

Many retirees die before their great deferred adventures are completed, or even begun. My father's *magnum opus* is this house, and he's lived in it for more than a decade. He drew up the plans himself, handing them over to an architect friend to translate into professional designs. He borrowed a JCB from a local farmer to dig out the foundations. He got hold of the stone and roof slates from a church that was being demolished near his surgery in Earby (when he was seen high up in the roof helping lower slates to the lorry below, rumours began that the doctor was having money troubles now he'd retired and had taken a job as a labourer). He acquired some Canadian pine from a neighbour, transported it to an old mill in Colne where he treated and sawed and planed it to make beams and shelves and doors and pot rails and dados, then brought it home and polyurythaned each item three times. He appointed a builder to begin the work, but also appointed himself foreman and chief helper. He chose the windows—metal, double-glazed, openable both side and top. He himself bought—'so there's no mark-up'—the copper pipes, the electrical fittings, the insulation wool, the roof felt, the wash-basins, the carpets, the lino, the pale-blue bath with the scraped side, at a knock-down price.

All those years of helping others with their golf club or pub dining-room extensions—projects quietly resented by my mother because time given to others was time denied to the family; all his long history of odd-jobbing—changing tap washers, fixing the electrics, lying with his ear to a blocked drain and coming up with his arm sleeved in sewer-black mud: all that had been mere practice for his greatest project, this house. Impatient and cheapskate, he was no craftsman. If a way could be found to get by with bits and pieces he already had, then he would find it, and fudge it, and bugger the appearance. Why buy a triangular corner cupboard when you could saw up a rectangular kitchen cabinet and have *two*? He was the sort of man who would raid his own skip, in case something useful had been chucked. Most of his tools are old, handed down from his father and grandfather and uncles; here they are, handle upward, in tubs of oil and sand to stop them rusting. I stand in the garage and workshop gazing at these testimonies to a practical man, the pliers and chisels and all the other things he'd picked up over the years ('How much for cash?') and could not bear to throw away: crumpled cans of Simoniz, paint tins with a crust-hard quarter-inch in the bottom, hanging saws with their teeth torn out, garden shears open like lobster claws, the drum circle of an extension lead, a knapsack weed-killer spray, a paraffin-wick road lamp, an oil can with its plunger jammed half out. Two tyres stand upright against the wall, a buffer to the front bumper of his car. There's a vice bolted to the workbench with nothing in its grip. His spanners and screwdrivers dangle in rows, getting bigger as they go. Above them are neat shelves of Senior Service or Golden Virginia tins with 'three-quarter inch brass screws' or 'one-inch galvanized nails' labelled on the side. Some day all these will be mine.

It took two winters in gloves and blue overalls, two summers in a pair of shorts, before he finished the house. He held a party to celebrate and gave the house a name— Windyridge, the name of the house he'd grown up in, an even apter name here, for a site where the wind never stops. That evening he sat back in his chair while the sun went down and the sky pinkened on the screen of hills from the Trough of Bowland to Upper Wharfedale. Next morning he began work on the garden: the lawn, the orchard, the vegetable plot, the summer house (built from leftovers, and resembling a bus shelter), the rockery, the orchard, the polyhouse. He was especially proud of the 'geriatric' flower-beds I'm wandering among now, the earth at waist height, so that he—or more likely my mother—need never bend while weeding.

He'd have liked me to help with his house, to be the apprentice, the plumber's mate, the Lad at his side. But I was lazy, and living two hundred miles away, and he roped in others instead—my brother-in-law Wynn (an employee of Yorkshire Water, good on the heavy work), my Uncle Ron (who brought to carpentry all his dentistry skills), neighbours, former patients, friends. I feel guilty now for not having been there; I feel guilty for ever having grown up and away. Often enough, at various addresses, he'd helped me. In one flat we'd constructed a door and wooden bridge from the bathroom out to the back garden, which was otherwise reached only by traipsing round through the curmudgeonly downstairs neighbour's yard: the bridge was made from two old railway sleepers snapped up on the cheap and transported down from Yorkshire, and the neighbour so hated their bulk and ugliness that he pleaded with us to take the bridge down and feel free to use his yard. Help of this sort meant my father storming ahead, and me standing at his side holding tools. So when it came to building his house, I couldn't reciprocate: I'd looked on but never learned his practical skills.

Besides, I missed the old rectory and selfishly resented him moving from a place I'd assumed would always be there to return to, a childhood I could pick up again if ever I fancied. And I recoiled from the new house precisely because it was new, which meant vulgar. Whenever I came up he would drag me away from whatever I was reading and escort me round his work in progress. I'd try to make approving noises, but below them was a lofty silence: I knew there were better ways for me to employ my time, and—sticking my head back in the nearest book—I probably conveyed the thought that there were better ways for him to employ his. Now, chastened and frightened, I want to tell him I was wrong—that it didn't matter any more to me that the only book I'd ever seen him reading (abandoned halfway through) was *Jaws*. I can see him with his head bowed over some faulty electrical appliance or blocked carburettor ('We'll soon fettle that'), lost and absorbed and self-transcending. Why had I thought my interests more important, less ephemeral than his? What could I compare with this monument he'd built to himself? What consolation can art be, what comfort are reading and writing, now that grief streams through the trees and this home he made for living in is about to become the house where he will die?

The wind gets up, flapping the plastic sides of the poly-house. I inhale the sweet air of tomato-and-compost, and see the brown plants shrivelled on the canes, and think of him tying them with green string and the first yellow bell-buds showing. It would have been June then. He would have been well, or would have thought he was well.

In Room 2, Ward 19, I want to shake him. I want to put a bomb under him. I want him to be dead rather than die like this.

'I know you don't feel right, Dad, but operations take it out of people, they feel flat afterwards, and you are much stronger than you were three days ago.'

'I am that.'

'And the doctors are happy. And once you're eating properly and in your own home . . .'

I don't know whether this blather is for his sake or mine —because it's the sort of cheeriness he goes in for himself and feels comfortable with; or because I can't bear to admit he's dying. I know they have opened him up and closed him again without doing anything other than pass a tube across his stomach. I know this can't help him regain his appetite or health. I know that if he doesn't start peeing soon, his kidneys will become infected, then pack up altogether. And I know that he knows all this, knows too much about the body to be deluded. Physician, diagnose thyself: well, he has, and that's why he's depressed.

'And you might not feel like visitors now, but there are lots of friends who want to see you, and in a week you'll be different.'

He looks at his watch and says: 'Number One, your five minutes are up. Come in Number Two. Your five minutes are up too, Two. Come in Number Three . . . No thanks.'

It is the only flash of something like anger, or life. No, of course he wouldn't want anyone to see him like this. He hates feeling fallible: 'I may not be right but I'm never wrong' is the motto on a horrible brass wall-plate he has. He isn't a vain man, but he is a proud, even bumptious one, a man with a puffed chest who learnt to water-ski in his fifties and thought he could go on forever. To be stalled and stranded like this is bad enough; for others to see him in this condition . . .

Lunch arrives at eleven-thirty, an omelette and mashed potatoes. He asks for some butter to moisten the food ('It's like swallowing holly, or iron spikes'). The television's on in the background, and there's a shot of Arthur Scargill from the archives. My father has never liked sharing a name with the miners' leader; he prefers if anything to be called 'King Arthur', the nickname some of his friends use in recognition of a certain tendency to lord it, or more-than-lord-it, over the locals. Now I want to delude him into recovering some of that bullying energy. I've seen him angry, in tears, petulant, sorry for himself, but never like this, never *down*.

My mother leaves us for a moment: 'Have a last word before the train.' I offer to lift him from the chair on to the bed, but he doesn't want to be lifted—'Soon as I'm up there, I'm bound to have to get down for a piss or shit.' He asks me only to pull the sheet back, too weak even for this. I hold him close a minute and feel the unfamiliar juttiness of his bones. I hold him a bit longer, not wanting him to see my face. I turn a last time at the door, but he is staring into space in front of him, or at the Thing inside him, not at me. I walk with my mother through the swing doors of Ward 19 and out into the drizzle, the gauze of dampness, which doesn't move at all, just hangs there helplessly, as if the sky cannot relieve itself or cry.

On Keighley station I recognize the older brother of one of my schoolfriends, or think I do. A young girl is on his arm, while her sister and mother stand just behind. I take a seat on the train opposite them. A low industrial estate goes by, the pens of a sheep auction, bleached grass by a river. Yes, it's him all right, though behind his thick lenses he shows no sign of recognizing me. The girl is besotted: she leans her head on the shoulder of his brown leather jacket. How old is she? Eighteen? Twenty-two? I can see his wedding ring, and I imagine what he may have gone through over the last weeks or months or years: an angry, rejecting wife, children too maybe. Then I imagine it differently: his cruel northern obduracy and heavy drinking and culture-licensed irresponsibility. I struggle between these two images.

What is his name? At Ermysteds, his brother Brian had been the most powerful figure in our year, clever, subversive, a fighter. Most of us suffered humiliations from him at one time or another: when I was twelve and overweight, I'd been sitting in the art room failing to paint and looked out of the window to find him holding up a piece of paper that said 'Fat PB'—P. B. being the initials (Philip Blake) the teachers used to distinguish me from R. A. Morrison, the red-haired boy I'd seen crying on my first morning in the playground (crying not because it was a scarily big new school but because he was a poor boy without a uniform). Fat PB became a nickname and taunt for a while. My parents, at whose insistence my sister and I would eat up all the helpings they served us, had let us both get 'chubby', their word for *fat*. They thought I'd grow out of it naturally. Maybe I would have. But I expect I have Brian to thank that I put myself on a diet and lost a stone in six weeks.

Brian was attractive to girls, and the first of us to get on to them. He got me on to them, too, but not literally and rather later than him. At fourteen, he and I double-dated—his of course was the prettier. I remember sitting awkwardly with mine (Janice? Helen? Linda?) under the girder of light in the local Plaza, the six-fifteen performance because she had to be home by nine. In a heat engendered more by classroom talk than by desire I tried to put my hand on her breasts, what there was of them, before realizing that convention required me to kiss her first, not easy, I discovered, when a girl keeps her face fixed firmly on the big screen straight ahead. After a few more evenings of this, both of us pretending that the struggles in the dark were happening to someone else, which for all the intimacy we achieved they might as well have been, we took to talking through the films instead. We were useless touchers but good talkers, and might have gone out together longer. But one summer weekend when I was away Brian seduced her in an empty barn—or so he claimed, and even she spoke about rough hands and straw in her knickers. It was never the same between her and me after that. But I remained obsessed with Brian—who got all the best girls, or stole the best ones I had, or made me feel mine weren't worth stealing ('scrawny', 'no tits', 'tight as a nun's bum') for the rest of my adolescence.

And now here's his brother, also with a young girl, and I hear him saying: 'When we get there, you sit next to your mam.' The girl has the same olive skin and deep-set eyes as he does. Suddenly I realize the time-warp I'm in: this is not the predatory twenty-year-old, Brian's cocky brother; this is a man in his mid-forties out with his wife (the grey-haired woman opposite) and two teenage daughters. Why is one of those girls, fifteen or so when I look at her more closely, behaving like his lover? Simply because—doting, innocent, old-fashioned—she seems to like her dad? Is the sternness of his wife the jealousy and disapproval of a woman pushed to the side of her own life? Is it still OK for daughters to make up to their dads like this? I follow them as we get off at Leeds, the girl still on his arm, and strain to hear another snatch of conversation, grab another clue. But then they're gone in the crowd.

I wait for the King's Cross train. Was this how my sister had once been with her father? Do I want my own daughter to be like this with me when she's fifteen? I think of the coach I see every morning when I walk my son to his school bus: F SCOTT & DAUGHTERS it says on the side, and there is still a little shock in seeing that, in the provocative departure from & SONS and the idea of a liberal-minded coach-firm proprietor —a further shock in realizing that F SCOTT might not be a man at all. The days of fathers and sons are over: they've run the heredity business for themselves, have invested all their names and money in it, and now the fathers are dying and the sons not taking over and the whole shebang's in ruins. The women have been effaced for too long—like my mother, who encouraged my father and me to discuss money alone in the study, who let

51

him go to the bar or bank for her, who at mealtimes gave us men the bigger helpings. It is time for the women to come forward, time . . .

The London train is running late. I wander over to where the mail vans used to gather, scene of one of my father's great escape stories. He had come down to see me in London, a one-pound winter special return, and had arrived at the station with only five minutes to spare. The visitors' car park was full and so he had left his car—a sporty drop-head orange Fiat—parked among several Post Office vans. It was illegal, he knew, but he was rushing. Just how illegal he saw on his return: a posse of mail-vans enclosed it, a tight, red, get-out-of-this-one circle. Improvising quickly, he asked at Station Enquiries, 'Has anyone seen an orange sports car? It's mine, I have a set of keys for it, but my son was supposed to leave it in the car park and it's not there.' He was directed to a guard, and then to an angry trio of Post Office workers.

'Oh, Christ,' he said, when they escorted him to where, as he knew, the car was parked, 'the daft sod.'

'Student, is he?' one of the guards asked, calming down.

'Yep, bloody student,' my Dad said. 'Supposed to be clever. Prize fathead, if you ask me.'

He rang me that evening, exultant at this rare case of him using me rather than I him: 'You should have seen their faces: absolutely livid. There must have been ten mail-vans boxing me in. But by the time I left we were great pals. Best thing of all: they'd have charged three-fifty in the car park. And I didn't pay a penny.'

Back in London, on the Northern Line, going southward, I find the destination boards are getting ahead of themselves, as usual, over-optimistic, promising what they aren't going to deliver: MORDEN 3 MINS, it says, but after ten there's still no sign of the train. Instead of frustration, I feel a rare affection for this suspended time. But then I hear the inevitable growling and swelling in the tunnel, the sleek rat springing hyperactive and lethal from its trap. The carriage is full of men, every one a killer, brow-lines of rage and torment sculpted as if with hammer and chisel. Next to me is a close-cropped twenty-year-old in a leather jacket, with an AIDS INTERNATIONAL DAY sticker. He crouches by the pneumatic doors next to his dog, a beautiful grey velvety Weimaraner. The dog is nervous to be travelling in this thing, the rattling steel, the shaky floor. Every so often it gives a little howl, and when it does its leathered owner yanks on its collar and pulls its face hard up against his, staring it out, boss, disciplinarian, torturer. Silence, then another little howl, and this time he cracks its head hard against the door. More and longer silence, but then, just before he stands up to get out at Bank, the dog howls again and the boy leans into its face and bites it below the eye. It yelps in pain as they disappear through the door.

I am close to yelping myself now. A storm breaks across the city. At Lewisham station the tracks are under water, and as the train sits there I see a grey mouse in the wall below the opposite platform, flooded out of its home, trying to find a way down, balancing on a stone above the flood, panicking this way and that. At Blackheath I get off and move with the pedestrian bleepers, then cross the wide expanse of road in front of two cul-de-sacs. A black car is winking to turn in and starts to move. Head-down, I pretend not to see him but I can sense over my shoulder that he's keeping on coming. Suddenly the car is there at my shoulder, a Stanza: the driver taps his finger against his head, the you're-a-nutter gesture, then accelerates into the car-width between me and the pavement. He's trying to prove a point, not kill me, but already I'm running after him shouting, 'No, it's you who's mad, you fucking arsehole bastard.' I run a hundred yards up the road, still shouting. His Stanza's disappearing round the corner into the cul-de-sac, and I imagine catching him at its far end, his face whiting-out as he sees me through the glass, his hands whizzing to get the window up, but my arm is through and locked around his neck, dragging him out, or I'm up on the bonnet with an iron bar I've found, shattering the windscreen and in for the kill, like those IRA executioners with the off-duty soldiers who drove into a funeral march at Milltown cemetery, justice, a bullet through the head, the body dumped over a wall somewhere.

I stop running—a madman with a bag and briefcase ready to kill. I turn round, walk breathlessly up the hill and reach the road I live on, where, finally, a quarter of a mile from home, I start to cry.

Bolton Abbey

THE THURSDAY OF Whit week, my parents' afternoon off. On days like this, school holidays or bank holidays, we often drive up the Dales: drystone walls, no trees, and a wind whistling like winter in the telegraph wires. But today it's sunny and we've stayed in the valley, and now we're pulling into the car park, very crowded, at Bolton Abbey. A brown river churfles past the ruin. A line of stones picks its way across—silver buttons on a dead man's chest. Trout leap out of their bull's-eyes to snatch up flies. I ask if we can get out and play here, but my father says, 'No, let's find somewhere quieter,' and off we go, past the Strid (just a step across the churning water, but if you slip you never come up again) and on towards Burnsall. My mother has gone shopping in Harrogate. Auntie Beaty is with us instead.

She's not my real Auntie, but my father calls her that because he says she is almost family. He met her three or four years ago, when she and her husband Sam became managers of the golf club. When my parents go to pubs, my sister and I have to stay in the car, with lemonade and crisps. But at the golf club we can wander off down the fairways looking for lost balls, or play in the yard at the back. I like the yard, the crates of empties stacked under the steamy kitchen window, the wasps you have to mind out for in the orangeades and Britvics. My parents stay a very long time inside, at the bar, where Auntie Beaty or Uncle Sam serves them. Once everyone was very merry and invited us in and we had shandy, and also onion and sugar sandwiches, which are much nicer than you think they're going to be.

When he has time for a round of golf as well as the bar, my father lets me caddy for him. I wheel his trolley over the frizzed grass, past larks' nests, the ball like a tiny white ulcer in the mouth of a bunker or green. There is one hole, the sixth, where we always see a lapwing, also known as a peewit or plover says the *Observer Book of Birds*. It's a lovely black and white colour, with a crest like one of Auntie Beaty's black curls. When we trundle the clubs past, it flies up, making terrible cries, as if it had been hurt or had lost something, and then suddenly it crashes to the ground and rolls and flops about with a broken wing. My father says not to be fooled, that it's perfectly healthy and knows what it's doing, and all its playacting is for just one thing—to lead us away from the nest. Once it flew straight at Uncle Gordon's head when he hit his second shot into the rough—he had got too close to the nest and it was desperate to scare him off.

'Why do we spend so much time with Auntie Beaty?' I asked once when we were driving back over the moors.

'Because she's a bit sad, and needs help,' he said.

'Why?'

'For one thing, she and Uncle Sam can't have children. And they also have money troubles.'

'Do you give them money?'

'I help with their accounts, so they'll learn to understand money and look after it themselves.'

But they can't have learnt to look after money yet, because

he is still there most nights till very late, and today Auntie Beaty has come out driving with us, and is sitting in the front of the car holding Josephine while my sister Gill and I sit in the back. Josephine—Josie—is nearly two now, and noisy, and has red cheeks and curly black hair. I can remember the day she was born. My father took my sister and me along to the maternity hospital, Cawder Ghyll: we couldn't go in, so he held us high at the window nearest Auntie Beaty's bed on the ground floor, and we saw the cot with the black head in it. Josie had been a surprise, and my father said we didn't have to feel sorry for Auntie Beaty and Uncle Sam any more: their troubles might not be over, but they had children now, which was a blessing. My mother wasn't there that day, though Cawder Ghyll was the hospital she delivered babies at, and she had delivered Josie too.

Auntie Beaty comes to our house a lot. Once I walked into the bathroom when she was feeding Josie: it felt funny, as if I shouldn't be there, but she didn't mind, and I saw her big white breast and the brown nipple when Josie took her mouth away. Another day she brought her Dad with her, Josie's grandpa: he stood at the edge of the raised bottom lawn, where the aubrietia climbs up the wall on to the paved edgings, and suddenly he tipped backwards and fell on his back on the gravel three feet below. He lay there, flat and white and gasping like a fish, and Auntie Beaty screamed, but my father came running with his little bag and helped him up and said it was all right, he must have lost his balance, it wasn't a heart attack. Auntie Beaty has been coming round even more since then. She is always laughing and my father is always laughing, though not my mother. Sometimes Auntie Beaty is kind, gives me crisps and sherbet fountains, hugs me till I taste the perfume on her neck and lets me test how springy her black curls are. But other times Gillian and I say we're fed up playing with Josie, and my

57

mother is sarcastic. Then my father gets cross and says we're all family and helping Beaty, and where's the harm?

I'm getting bored now in the back of the car, even though the roof's down, our hair in our faces. I'm in training for the Olympics, the hundred, the two hundred, the four hundred, the high jump, the long jump. At last year's village fête in our paddock, I came next to last in the under-nines dash, but I know I can do better this year. It was a bad day for other reasons. My mother had her terrible migraine, and maybe that affected my performance. I think it was my worst day ever— worse than when she skidded on the cow-muck and crashed the car; worse than when she ran screaming up the stairs because the wardrobe had fallen on top of Gillian; worse than when I was made to stay in bed all day as a punishment for still at my age dirtying my pants. I came back to the house after the tug-of-war and heard a noise from upstairs. She was moaning and rolling about on the bed, holding the back of her hand to her forehead. 'Get Daddy, quick,' she said, and I fetched him from the raffle, fast. I waited downstairs, then another doctor from the hospital came, and they told me to go back to the fête. At least I beat Christine Rawlinson in the race, but I should have beaten Stephen Ormrod as well. When I got back Lennie, the maid, said 'It's all right, she's at peace now,' and I thought she must mean: Your mummy's dead. She wasn't, and has had only two migraines since, but I worry that she might roll and moan with another strong one. In the Bible, when David is a boy, before meeting Goliath, he plays his harp at the court and the King's headaches disappear. I wish I could cure my mother's migraines like that, but I can only play the piano, and Mrs Brown says I need more practice before I can take Grade One. I think curing migraines is probably a much higher grade, Nine or Ten at least.

My father has turned off the lane on to a grass-seamed

track between two gateposts. He parks the car, the handbrake clicking tight, the silence after the ignition key. We are at the top of a hill, above a rough meadow with thistles and butter-cups and cow-parsley.

'Why don't you and Gill take Josephine down the hill,' he says. 'You'll be all right—just hold her hand. We can watch you from here.'

'Oh, Arthur, I'm not sure,' says Auntie Beaty.

'No, go on, they'll be fine,' he says. 'Lovely day, no sheep or cows to worry them, wonderful spot for children. Blake will look after her: he's nine now. Everything will be fine. Where's the harm?'

So we walk down the meadow, Josie's small hand trust-ingly in mine, which makes me feel big and in charge. I want to turn round to make sure my father and Auntie Beaty are watching us, but I don't. I'm not like Lot's wife in the picture at Sunday school. I'll show them I can be trusted.

On the level ground at the bottom of the field, there's nothing much to do, but I know we shouldn't turn back straight away. Gill begins to pick buttercups. Josie sits down on her terry-and-plastic bottom. She's too small to play games. I wish my father were here to sprint against. A lapwing wheels away from us, rising then plunging, and I think: 'Enough of your tricks. I know your nest is near. I could smash every egg if I tried.' I've learnt a lot about birds lately. We have a redstart's nest in the wall below the billiard-room. There was a pied wagtail on the lawn this morning, headbobbing and lifting its skirt, putting food in the mouth of its chick, which was fluffy and even bigger than its mother and should be fending for itself by now. And that distant cry just now was a curlew's, I think, getting faster and higher.

I look up the field to where the car's parked, but the windscreen is lit and flaring and I can't see behind it. It's as if all the power of the sun were in the glass containing Dad and Auntie Beaty, and no one else can look on it without being blinded. I put my hand—flat, as if saluting—over my eyes, and look again. I think I can see two heads there, close together, safe inside the blaze. I wait for the car doors to open, and I hear my father's voice again: 'Everything will be fine. Where's the harm?'

Foetal

ON TUESDAY EVENING, three days after I've left him in Ward 19, my mother rings while he's asleep to say that I'm not to know this, that I must feign amazement and let him be the one to tell me, but he's home. I wait till ten for his call, but it doesn't come, so in the end it's me who rings and she who answers and he who picks up the extension by his bed. For years now, when you call one of my parents, you speak to both. In the early days, before extensions, he got himself an earpiece, so while my mother stood with the phone he'd be there listening alongside and shouting comments until in the end she gave up and changed places and he took over. Then came British Telecom, and a phone in every room, and dialogues for three voices.

'You're home, Dad.'

'I thought that might surprise you.'

'He wanted it to be a surprise.'

'Well it is a surprise. How you feeling?'

'A bit better now. Sharp pain under the scar, but you know that old theory—if a child has tummy pains, put a penny on its umbilicus and tie a bandage round.'

'He says it's working a treat.'

'You have a penny on your umbilicus?'

'Not a penny, a tight bandage. And I've slept fourteen hours today.'

'He needs the rest.'

'That's good,' I say, though it isn't and he doesn't, not on that scale. My father sleeping fourteen hours a day? The man who reckoned he needed only six hours and a couple of catnaps? Come *on*.

'I'm glad to be back.'

'He's among his own things, that helps.'

'Great.'

'But no one else knows I'm home yet and I'm not telling.'

'He wants them to go on thinking he's in hospital.'

'Why?'

'So they won't visit me, that's why.'

I listen to his faded voice, and remember part of my conversation with Dr Taggart—'Can he die at home?' 'I don't see why not: your mother's a doctor, and there's nothing more we can do for him in hospital'—and wonder if this is where we've got already.

'So you're on the mend.'

'Aye, home now, can't be bad.'

'And he's got me to look after him.'

'Can I can come up and see you?'

'You've just gone back. You don't want to bother.'

'He's still weak: he needs to take it easy.'

'Soon, though.'

'When I'm better.'

'When he's stronger.'

'Too true.'

Three days later, a red sun sinking over Cambridgeshire and Lincolnshire, I'm on the InterCity north again. The call had come this morning, while he was asleep: 'Better make it this weekend,' my mother says, 'just in case: I don't think it will be long.' Not long; it is only ten days since the cancer was confirmed.

Wynn, my brother-in-law, picks me up at Skipton station. 'Bad do,' he says. He hasn't been allowed to see my father yet —not flesh and blood. I tell him he must come in the house with me, but when we get there it seems to be shut up, derelict or in mourning. Thick curtains are drawn in the downstairs bedroom, and two plywood boards have been stuck over the front door glass. 'It's always like that these days,' says Wynn, 'to stop people looking in.' Never mind that the house stands in an acre of ground and is reached only by a long drive: there is still the postman, the milkman, the passing salesman. My father is taking no chances.

He is sitting in one of a pair of green reclining chairs that he bought a quarter of a century ago, the venue of his catnaps. The chair has a lever at the side to tip yourself back and bring up the footrest. Now, though, he's perched at the edge, leaning forward, head on his chest. He wears a pink shirt and green cardigan, nothing else. There is a white handkerchief bunched up between his thighs—his modesty rag, or figleaf. The bottom buttons of his shirt are undone, and his belly swells from it, a pregnant woman's belly, even down to the brown bisecting line that runs from top to bottom through the navel. I look again and see this isn't a line, but the zip of his scar (my three-year-old nephew is similarly deceived at first sight: 'What's that railway track on Grandpa's tummy?' he whispers). There is a little hernia bulge pushing through just above the navel, like some small object left beneath a carpet.

He shakes our hands wanly, raising his head a moment. 'As you can see, I'm bloody awful. From a fit seventy-year-old to a doddery ninety-year-old in a couple of weeks.' It's said not self-pityingly, merely to confirm that he too has grasped this indisputable truth—we mustn't pretend we can't see it.

There is a small milk stain on his lip and chin, and he keeps trying to belch. 'I feel so full, though I've not eaten for weeks. The things I need to help me belch I don't fancy at all.' But he tries, over the next hour: a sip of fruit juice; an egg beaten with sherry; a swig of my mother's Liebfraumilch. 'Swig,' he says, leaning back in his chair, eyes closed, 'funny word, swig.' Under his head is the red tartan blanket that he's had since my childhood, maybe since his childhood, that we took to the annual point-to-point races at Gisburn, and on other outings, and spread out for the creaking picnic-basket. As we talk, a circling talk of family, Christmas, local scandal, his eyes remain closed and he seems to be asleep, but then he pipes up and it's clear he's been taking it all in. He has his hands folded behind him, but sometimes he removes them and holds them raised above his head, right-angled at the elbows, palms flat, as if supporting some great weight. From time to time he asks me to make minute adjustments to the rug behind his head, to double-fold or quadruple-fold, to raise or lower. I stand behind his thinning head, and catch the grass-and-earth reek of the rug, and remember lying wrapped in it myself, late at night, coming home in the back of the Alvis, the murmur of my parents' voices from the front, my eyes closed just as his eyes are now, the luxury of being borne swaddled and trusting and unseeing through the night.

Suddenly he tips his chair forward. The handkerchief scrunched between his thighs falls to the floor, and I see his penis scrolled up in its sac, a sad little rose, no engorgement. I remember how big it seemed when I saw it as a child at the swimming baths, and how I looked forward to being an adult so I could have one that big too. I think how as adult heterosexual males we rarely see each other's penises and never see each other's erections—least of all our fathers' erections—and I catch myself grieving that he may never have an erection again. Then I think how embarrassing these thoughts are. I pick up his modesty rag and hand it to him and he stows it gently back in place.

When he talks, his conversation is of a characteristic count-your-blessings kind.

'I'm bloody lucky, you know. I have you here, and Gill next door, and Pat and Mummy. Marvellous.'

Or: 'If our purpose on this earth is to make it a better place for our children, then we haven't done badly.'

Or: 'I'm a little better today than I was yesterday. And yesterday than the day before. And the day before than the day before that.'

He talks himself up like this all evening. He extols the virtues of the new portable telephone he bought for 129 pounds just before going into hospital—'you can take it two hundred yards down the garden—it'll be useful when I'm lying out in summer, or next back-end when I'm raking leaves.' He tells me about the new headlamps he's ordered for when he's fit to drive again, for when he goes back to hospital to have his stitches out in a couple of weeks. There is tenacity in all this denial, some deep will to survive, and we collude in it. My mother teases him—'We've not had him climbing any hills yet, but tomorrow maybe'—and runs her fingers through his hair. I imagine him reaching Christmas at any rate, two and a half weeks away—wrapped in his red tartan blanket smiling bravely while the children open their presents, sad to think there may be no more Christmases but appeased by the joy and continuity around him. I had come up half-ready to spend longer than the weekend here, but there's no immediate panic. At ten he goes to bed, tottering off like a toddler in its mother's high-heeled shoes. I ring my wife and tell her to expect me the following evening.

*

I wake next day around six-thirty, my father's deep voice rising comfortingly from downstairs, an echo of my childhood and all its other morning noises—the door unlatched to let the dog out for a pee, the row of milk sentries set chinkingly on the window-sill, the kettle crescendo-ing on the Aga. I read and then run a bath and bolt the door. For the past week my stomach has been bothering me, slight pain and swelling, as if—just as my father had claimed to feel belly pains when my mother was in labour—I were trying to share his cancer, the ties that bind, my filial couvade. But today I'm feeling better. The hot water laps over my stomach and thighs. I think of the behind-locked-doors furtiveness of adolescence, and the thought, or the soapy water, arouses me, because I'm hard now, and start to masturbate, wondering if this is wrong and something I should feel guilty about, in the midst of death and with my father downstairs, but wanting the escape, reluctant to let the feeling pass. Now little white snakes swirl in the water, and Sylko threads snag against my skin. They turn to jelly first, then dry on me in a flaky glaze. I get out and swill the bath with the shower-head. The sky is a misted blue over Pendle Hill, and sheep are passing slowly over the cold fields.

But my mother, fetching me tea, is close to tears.

'I'm worried, love. He woke at six and was violently sick —nasty brown stuff, what we call foetal vomiting.'

'What's that?'

'Well, it's basically sicking up your own excrement. It's usually a terminal sign.'

'But he seemed all right.'

'Yes, but he took three sleeping-pills in the night, so he says, and he's all doped and doolally now. I need your help to move him.'

He is sitting on the edge of the bed, his favourite hunched-forwards position to get wind up. He's out-of-breath and looks a decade older than last night, his eyes yellowed over and misty.

'How are you, Dad?'

'Bloody rough. Pig sick.'

'But you were bright enough last night.'

'I was that.'

I swing his legs up on to the bed, and then my mother and I take an arm and an armpit each and try to slide him up on to the pillows. It's like moving a heap of rubble, and when we finally get him there he's asleep at once. We don't know whether to believe his story about the sleeping-pills or if this is a sudden catastrophic decline. My mother shows me the sheet he was sick into, the dark brown stain on it, not smelling of shit, but looking like it.

We consult his chart, pages 622 and 624 of an old ledger he has torn out so as to record his regime of pills and injections and food intake—the old workhorse. He has drawn extra rules down and across the chart, so densely that it looks like a pools coupon: Redoxon, Amiodarone, Heparin, Valium, Maxolon, Diconal, Paracetamol, Frusemide, Periactin, Complan, Eggs, Cereal, Chivas Regal, Water. It's neat and fanatical, just like all the other endless lists and diagrams and instruction sheets he's compiled over the years, and with the same message: he's in control. But the last few entries are in my mother's writing, not his: *he* can no longer hold a pen. And we can't tell from his notes how many Diconal he had earlier in the week and how many should be left—there are forty-seven in the bottle, but did he really take three in the night?

He is still asleep at eleven, when a car draws up. A middle-aged man gets out, the car bleep-bleeping as he locks it. An AIREDALE HOSPITAL plastic identity tag pendulums on his lapel: the consultant, Dr May. My father has looked forward to this visit for days and wakes at once, rousing himself from death, talking lucidly about exactly which drugs he's taken, how many milligrams, and how he thinks a change in dosage will help his progress. Dr May listens, takes his pulse, checks his temperature, taps his finger against his chest.

'Your back now,' he says, which means moving my father forward off the pillows. I hold him by the wrists and palms, feeling their gentle jolts and convulsions, the life in him flickering like one of his old cine films.

'We need to give you some more Frusemide, Arthur, which will help you get your appetite back. And there's a little water on your abdomen, which is pushing your diaphragm up and making you nauseous, so I'll give you something to get rid of that. In a couple of days your guts should be working better. I'll visit again then.'

But this optimism is for my father, not us. Dr May has seen the sheet, and in the dining-room he tells us: 'It's not good. He's very poorly. We're talking days, I think, not weeks.'

'You think it's faecal vomiting, then?'

'It looks like it.'

He bleeps his car door open and drives away. *Faecal* vomiting, I realize she just said, not *foetal*. Had I misheard it earlier because I didn't want to hear it right, because I wanted associations of birth not death? 'Foetal' had made me think of meconium, the black stuff during labour when a baby is in distress, the shit in the womb which midwives and doctors recognize as a signal for a forceps delivery or Caesarean. My father's, too, is shit voided into a stomach, violating places where it shouldn't be. He, too—the great moment approaching —is a baby in distress.

Camp Cuba

SUNDAY BREAKFAST IN the dining-room, the sun riding down from Embsay Moor. My father has recently bought a freezer and his paean to frozen food sounds as if it's been scripted by an ad agency: 'Just think, these raspberries we're eating were picked three months ago. And they taste as if I'd brought them in this morning. Marvellous. None of that metallic sogginess you get from tins. Incredible thing, science.' The raspberries are a rich purple, paled and mottled by sugar. There is All-Bran or Weetabix to follow, from the same deep-blue bowl we have had the raspberries in ('Must save on washing up for Mummy'). On the side-plates my father has laid out a series of vitamin pills: he has become fanatical about minding his As and Bs, his Cs and Ds, newly convinced that we can avoid colds and flu if we adopt a regime of tablets and capsules. Some of the pills are hard to swallow, others star-burst oilily when you nip their skin with your teeth. The family, not for the first time, is acting as a controlled medical experiment: what we are swallowing today, every patient in Earby will be swallowing tomorrow.

It is hard to reconcile this health regime with the next course, the bacon, egg, tomato and dippy bread—a slice of white bread frizzled in the leftover fat in the frying-pan. 'You

69

can't beat dippy,' my father says as he slides the last piece of it around his plate, soaking up yet more heart-gunge, yet more killing fluids. Dippy is the last of the bad old fat habits to go—even after butter has been replaced by margarine, it passes muster. Once, we used to consume the hot fat on chops, the crackling on pork, the white lard-edge on cold beef, the fat-smeary blood-juice of a roast joint. This was more than just the house rule about 'finishing everything on your plate': fat, I was told, would 'get some strength in you.' By now my father is cholesterol-conscious, and no one is pretending that dippy bread is good for you. Still, we're eating it.

After toast and marmalade, my father and I retire to the two tip-back chairs which face out through the sash windows towards the moor. He is checking the share market, I the sports pages of the *Sunday Express*, where I stare for hours at the blurred anguish of a backward-arching goalkeeper as a shot from Burnley's Ray Pointer (white dotted arrows painted on the photo to trace its path) inflates the net behind him—for me at twelve, the ultimate erotica: the breast-like bulge of a top corner. My mother, having cleared the breakfast stuff, is back again now with two mugs of coffee: 'Made with hot milk, Mummy? Smashing.'

It is my father who says this, not me. All through our childhood he has called his wife 'Mummy', never Agnes, her actual name, which he hates because it sounds drab and old-fashioned, never Kim either, the name her friends use and which he persuaded her to adopt not so much to seem chic and fifties—was it plagiarized from Kim Novak?—as to erase her rural Irish past. She has shed her name, abandoned her country and buried her Kerry accent; in return he calls her 'Mummy'. Until now, it has sounded fine, but at twelve it's beginning to embarrass me: I want to call them Mum and Dad, which is what my schoolfriends' parents are called, but which they think 'common'; and I want them to call each other Kim (or even Agnes) and Arthur. It's a futile ambition. My father will never change his habits. He'll go on calling her Mummy—'Glass of wine, Mummy, love?'—long after my sister and I have left home. He'll call her Mummy with increasing frequency once his own mother dies. And he'll call her Mummy not just in front of her grown-up children but in the company of friends, strangers in pubs, even when they are alone.

'It's your half-term coming up,' he says.

'Hum.'

'I've been thinking. It's time we went camping.'

'Camping?'

'You know, fathead—tent, poles.'

'Hum.'

'Just the two of us, boys together—or *men* together.'

I have just had my twelfth birthday. This is what he must mean by 'men'. The thought of a camping holiday with my father fills me with dread.

'We could go to the Lakes. Just us. The girls could drive up and join us for a meal out together at the end.'

'Hum.'

'It's good to get away sometimes, you know—we love Mummy and Gillian, but there are things we're better off doing on our own, no faffing about or worrying if they're cold: you can't imagine them enjoying three nights in a tent like we will.'

'Hum.'

'Under the stars, fresh air and exercise—marvellous.'

A week later, on a hill above Lake Windermere, we're listening to the six o'clock news: there is something about Fidel Castro, with his big beard, and President Kennedy, who is so young and smily and perfect, and President Khrushchev, who my father says you can't trust. 'Secret installations', the newsreader says several times, and I think how difficult it must be to hide bombs: I have seen pictures of them and they are huge, or at least the clouds they give off are huge. Below, a rowing-boat chops and stitches its way across the water. The sheep on the green hills opposite are dotted tinily up to the summit, then evaporate into cumuli. 'Marvellous,' my father says. 'Couldn't have picked a better day. Fresh air, blue sky, not a soul in sight—makes you glad to be alive.'

I sit on the tartan rug while he reaches into the boot, then dumps the heavy, rope-necked canvas swagbag on to the turf beside me. He undoes the rope, then slides the bag along the length of tent and yanks it up, like a mother removing the dungarees from her flat-on-its-back, nappy-heavy toddler. It must be years since the tent was last up, on the beach at Abersoch or in the back garden, but at once a familiar smell rises from it—the smell of canvas and sand-dunes and grass cuttings and suntan oil and dead earwigs.

'Funny,' my father says, and goes back to the boot of the car. I get up, and fiddle with the guy-ropes, their heavy wooden adjustables.

'Is there a bag anywhere under the tent?' he shouts, as he opens the car door and peers under the back seat. I lift one corner and find a small blue canvas holdall.

'Yes,' I call.

'What's in it?'

'Pegs,' I shout back, pulling out a clunky handful of them —they look like primitive-man sticks of firewood, with little notches axed into the side.

'No poles?'

'No.'

I can remember what the poles are like—thick, wooden, three feet long, with large metal spears and slots at each end.

I search the bracken, the canvas, under the car.

'I must have put them in,' my father says, without conviction.

'Couldn't we break some branches off and make do with those?'

'Don't be daft. It'll be dark in half an hour.'

'What are we going to do?'

'Pack up and go home.'

On the drove-road back down, though, he has another idea. 'We could stay in a hotel, I suppose. And ring Mummy, and get her to drive up with the poles tomorrow and meet us halfway.'

Monday evening, with poles. After the misfortune of the night before—soon enough converted by my father into a huge joke against himself, the sort he could afford once he'd found the cosy hotel, with its log fire, consommé and roast duck—we have spent most of the day in the car. First we drove to meet my mother and sister in Kirkby Lonsdale, and had lunch. Then we came north again, nosing through the drizzle round Grasmere and Rydal Water, listening to the car radio, the weather forecast, the latest on Cuba. 'It's bound to clear up soon,' my father says, who is never one to complain, whose meteorology is a science of optimism. To him, rain is the natural order of things, which in the Yorkshire Dales is about right, and anything other than rain is a blessing. 'Lucky with the weather,' he'll say when it's heavy and overcast. 'Marvellous day' denotes high cloud. 'Miraculous, like being on the Riviera' is when the sun, however briefly, gets through the clouds.

At five we begin looking for a good pitching spot—'I suppose there are official sites, but it's not the same as camping wild, and you have to pay.' We drive to Ambleside and

Windermere: nothing. We take a left turn to Skelwith Bridge: the fields by the river are fenced off with barbed wire. We go back to Grasmere, through Chapel Stile, to the Dungeon Ghyll Hotel (trying not to notice the word Hotel), and as darkness begins to fall we settle on a spot by a stream. It is a low, unsheltered strip of flat grass. The sky above us is threatening heavier rain than this mild fuzz. Already I'm nostalgic for the site we found last night, but to which my father says it would be 'bad luck' to return. The farmer, though apparently surprised when we ask, has no objection to our being here. And it is a good spot to begin walking from tomorrow, up to Harrison Stickle and the Langdale Pikes. As my father's torch dims from a bright stare to yellow myopia—'Bloody batteries gone already' —we get the last guy-rope secured, the last bendy leg of the camp-bed into its slot. It is only, what, seven-thirty, but I want to climb into my sleeping-bag.

We tie the tent flaps and set off for the pub, leaving the shaky house by the stream. As we drive, the Home Service is taken up with Presidents Kennedy and Khrushchev: the smily young hero has blockaded Cuba; Russian ships are sailing towards it. There are words I don't understand—diplomatic manoeuvres and retaliatory risks—and words that need no explanation, like World War Three. Will my father be too old to fight this time? I've had this daydream for years that if he's called up for war we'll keep him in the attic, like that picture I've seen at school of the Cavalier concealed in a tree-trunk. And if they send someone looking for him and ask me do I know where he is, when did I last see him, could they just look round, I'll not give him away, I'll keep his secret safe . . . Now the next war's nearly here, though, my plan seems childish. Maybe this time no one will have to fight, it can all just be push-buttons. We slam the car doors and step into the pub car park. Annihilation must look like the sky does now, blindness

and blackness. And serving in a war must feel like this—
a strange place at night, the home you live in irretrievably
vulnerable and far away.

It's quiet inside, and the barman doesn't seem to notice my
juniority (does he take me for fourteen? eighteen? is he pretending not to see?). The warmth and cigarette smoke and
sawdusty floorboards create a fug of sociability, but it's hard to
settle into, knowing we have to drive back to the cold tent,
knowing the world may end. There are only men in here, big,
smoking, laughing men jawing about war.

'Them bloody Russkies need a taste of their own medicine,'
says the fat one with sideboards from his bar-stool. 'This
Kennedy's called their tune. He's the first to stand up to 'em like
we should have long since. I take my hat off to him.'

'Nay, Frank,' says the barman, 'the Reds an't been that
bad. They've not dropped their bombs on anyone.'

'Maybe so, but they've got as far as Cuba, and this Castro
bugger is standing there with open arms saying come on in,
there's plenty room for thee, you can hide your nuclear
weapons in my beard.'

'It's a Communist country, Frank, Cuba is, and there's no
law against making friends with Russians. It were them who
invented Communism.'

'Nay, tha's wrong there, it were Karl Marx what invented
Communism, and he lived in England. Great beard on him,
too. I tell you, if we don't stop these Commies pointing their
weapons at us, we'll all be for the chop.'

'What a world it's coming to,' my father pipes up from our
pock-marked brass table by the log fire, shaking his head,
hoping some neutral, uncontentious remark like this will let
him in on the conversation, will be the right kind of admission
fee. The fat man with sideboards shuts up now, the barman
goes off to serve another customer, and my father is left

hanging there, at the edge of someone else's talk, wanting to insinuate himself, to be accepted. I know how it will go from here, because it's happened before in other pubs. My father will pick up our glasses, order another pint, start chatting to the man in sideboards, buy me shandy and crisps and say: 'Marvellous part of the world: wish I knew it better. What's your poison? Theakstons?' I am beginning to miss my mother. I don't want to watch what's going to happen happening: my father slowly winning over the suspicious locals; the conversation turning from world politics to legends of local brawlers, womanizers, con artists; the pint after pint, the whisky chasers, then the one for the road, and the next one for the road and the last one for the road. I stare at the smoke rising from the logs and imagine one wisp of it journeying up the chimney and out through the stack into the night, to dissolve in the immense black spaces and be gone from sight if anyone were looking, and yet not be gone, for surely nothing can be lost forever, every trace of whatever happened on the earth is recorded somewhere, even the dimmest or shortest life must have its immortality: the stars are shooting us for someone.

It seems very late, but perhaps it's no later than closing time when we leave, my father belatedly guilty at the sight of me sitting alone by the fire, a collage of deconstructed beer-mats across the brass table. The cold drizzle in the car park comes as a shock, and as we drive back the radio spits and crackles over the whish-whosh of the wipers—'crisis', 'urgency', 'ultimatum'. Soon the headlights are picking out our frail little homestead: it looks like a story-book picture of the first pig's house, the one made of straw. The wind is getting up now, not to wolf-howl strength, but enough to growl and yank at the guy-ropes. We stoop inside, relieved to be out of the rain, but even my father's cheeriness can't make this a homely place, let alone home. He hands me a flask of coffee, with whisky added.

'That'll help you sleep,' he says, as my throat implodes, my stomach seethes with fission. I hear the rain beat the canvas. I hear the stream getting louder, more confident. I look up into the blackness and imagine Russian ships steaming across the dark sea and meeting American ships and all the bright final skies. There seems no kindly light that will lead us out of this, my father and me, here in our paper bag amid the encircling gloom.

We wake very early. The stream has burst its banks, and our tent, which has no groundsheet, is standing in an inch of water. I peer down and see water swishing about the metal legs of the camp-bed. My back feels damp, my bottom wet— it *is* wet, dunked where the camp-bed sags in the middle. Outside it's raining still and the wind whines to be off its leash. We drag ourselves out of our sleeping-bags and into our shoes, and splosh about in a sort of panic to be gone, breaking up the camp-beds, uprooting the pegs, dismantling the poles, tearing the canvas from its frame. It seems extraordinary, in the light of day, that we should have chosen this site—the stream looks higher than the fold of grass we pitched the tent in. But at least the tedious rituals of tent-packing can be dispensed with: we just dump the stuff higgledy-piggledy in the boot, and by eight o'clock are on the road, the fan of the car heater noisily combating our sogged gloom. 'We can dry the tent out later, spread it over some bushes while we have a picnic lunch,' says my father, peering through the metronome of the windscreen wipers.

We have two mixed grills ('Do you do dippy bread?') in a steamed-up Ambleside café, walk soddenly round the town, have lunch in a Patterdale pub. It stops raining round four— 'Told you our luck was in'—but it's too late by then to think of drying the tent, even if the sun had come out, which it hasn't. There's nothing to stop us putting it up damp, of course, which is what my father seems determined to do. He gets the map out. 'Got it, just the spot,' he says, and we drive on through more flooded lanes, damp hedgerows, mist-obscured fells. 'Must ring surgery,' he says, pulling up by a red telephone box, not for the first time on this holiday, or others. Surely it's too early for surgery? Who can he be ringing? Through the mist of panes, I can see his head nodding. Any sane person would have called it quits by now, would have turned round and gone home, but here we are, proving ourselves hardy and hearty, pointlessly.

An hour later, I am sitting in front of a hotel lounge fire. My father fetches me a whisky mac: 'You're all right, they'll not notice, it'll help you thaw out. My feet are like ice.'

'Thanks, Dad.' He is still gloating at the trick he has pulled on me—trick or treat, I'm not sure which.

'Happier now?'

'Yes.'

'Maybe it's soft, but I didn't see any point sleeping in that sodding tent with the forecast for more rain.'

'You're right.'

'And it is our last night, and we're still boys away together. If I'd been on my own, or with Uncle Ron, I'd have stuck it, but there was no point making you miserable—I sometimes forget, you *are* only twelve.'

I let this go, too relieved to be here to argue. There is a television in the corner of the room, a little grey window high in a walnut tower, and when the news comes on there are pictures of a smiling President Kennedy: the Russian ships have turned back, the newsreader says, and Mr Khrushchev has agreed to dismantle all his missile bases in Cuba. A man with a microphone stands in front of the White House and says: 'No one here yet knows what precisely made the Russians back down.'

My father and I clink glasses.

'Here's to Kennedy,' he says.

'To Kennedy,' I reply, my eyes watering over.

A Completely Different Story

MY FATHER IS asleep, and has been for hours. His rasping slowness and stiff-mouthed, dry-lipped wide-openness remind me of Terry Kilmartin, my old boss, three days before he died in the Lister hospital. Terry's had been a long, slow cancer, and on that last visit there seemed a peace and acceptance about him I hadn't seen during the pain-tautened months before. His freckled hand lay on the white deck and I held it, just as I've held my father's today: love, obeisance, the pupil paying respect to his mentor. But what sort of peace and acceptance is it that only morphine brings? I want my mentors back, awake and doubting.

On her long dressing-table stool at the end of the bed, my mother and I discuss funeral arrangements. We're nervous with each other, not sure if this is the right way to go about things, prefacing each new item—the wake, the will, what to do with his ashes—with 'I'm sorry, it sounds macabre, but . . . ' His dying is all we can think about, but is talking about it immoral, inauspicious, defeatist? She tells me how at his insistence she phoned the garage this morning to see if the new headlamps had come in and how they've just rung back and quoted seventy pounds—at which point my father wakes and says, 'I'm sure Halfords could do it cheaper,' then goes off again. We snigger at how the word *garage* sparked him into consciousness, whereas he'd slept through *coffin* and *crematorium*. Or is he just pretending not to hear? Mothers shut out the memory of childbirth pain once labour is over: my father has blanked off the diagnosis of ten days ago in much the same way. He can't hear the word *death* because he knows he's getting better.

I wander into his study. In one corner is the Amiga he acquired a year ago: in the last few months he's been teaching himself to type and word-process. In the opposite corner is his old drop-leaf desk, and above it, on the wall, a map of the West Riding, *circa* 1616, a barometer stuck between Fair and Changeable, and brass plates engraved with cheeky pub mottoes (A WOMAN'S BEST 10 YEARS ARE BETWEEN THE AGES OF 28 AND 30; IF YOU'RE SO DAMN SMART, WHY AIN'T YOU RICH?; EVERYTHING I LIKE IS IMMORAL, ILLEGAL OR FATTENING; A WIFE IS SOMEONE WHO STANDS BY HER HUSBAND THROUGH ALL THE TROUBLES HE'D NOT HAVE HAD IF HE HADN'T MARRIED HER; and, his catchphrase, I MAY NOT BE RIGHT, BUT I'M NEVER WRONG). In the middle of the desk is the letter he told me would be there, the one which he sat composing for three hours the day before I came, printed out on computer paper:

CONFIDENTIAL

Dear Drs,
I am writing to apologize for failing to keep you fully aquainted [*sic*]with updates of our medical history.

When Kim and I retired I decided that we would look after each other as far as possible without having to trouble you busy practitioners. I even prevailed upon consultants, many of whom are our personal— friends, not to forward any reports to Earby surgery—

particularly as we all know how rapidly news spreads around the 'grape-vine'—until WE gave the go-ahead.

That time now appears to have come!!!

About three and a half years ago, despite having no comlaint [*sic*], I went to Airedale, just to try out the Treadmill, and I was very disappointed to learn that I had an irregular heart action. I was heavily reassured that it would not affect my life expectancy, nor my day-to-day activity, gardening, etc. To ensure additional care I was fitted with a Dual Chamber Pace Maker.

This, above all, made me determined that no rumour 'Dr Morrison has a bad heart' [*sic*] and I continued to work and behave normally.

A year ago I developed auricular fibrillation and I was put on amiodarone 200 mgm daily, recovered rapidly and resumed my normal activities.

Now however I have a completely different story to tell. I have an adherent Splenic Obstruction with Ascites, now by-passed, and you will be getting full details via the post.

I do not require a visit, in fact I would hate one, at present—no offence intended.

Arthur B. Morrison

The letter is unsigned. I read it several times, then put it back as I found it.

Why had he contacted his GP now? Because he knew that to get your death-certificate signed, without first undergoing a post-mortem, you have to have seen a doctor in the previous twelve months? But surely a hospital doctor's signature would have done; besides, this letter specifically asked the local GPs not to visit him. Was it an atonement for his unprofessionalism? I could imagine him bollocking anyone who'd behaved as he had, who'd not been to his doctor for fifteen years—'You've been avoiding me: well, it's your funeral.' But mainly, I think, the letter was intended for us, the family: he had printed out three copies, and from time to time would ask me if I'd read it. Still denying in conversation how near to death he was, he had written the letter to acknowledge that he did know, and wanted us to know, and wanted us to know he knew.

Beneath the three printouts I find his medical card, the old brown National Health envelope with red ruled boxes on the front. It's been stamped twice—5 Jul 1948 in a circle and YN 24 Apr 1975 in an oblong. Inside is a single brown card and four new-looking, stapled-together letters: 1. 11 Oct 1991, confirming no abnormality at the Endoscopy Clinic but for a 'moderate-sized hernia'; 2. A discharge certificate dated 27.9.91 after an earlier investigation of 'bellyache'; 3. A letter from the Driver and Vehicle Licensing Centre in Swansea, acknowledging application for a driving licence but requesting details of any changes in his medical condition since his last application; 4. A letter of 28 November 1978 about a haemorrhoidectomy— 'Three primary piles (very large left lateral) and two secondary piles dissected up, ligated and removed.'

The card itself is terse—just twenty-two entries in forty-four years, seven of them to do with a lung infection in the long cold winter of 1962, and three others recording polio injections and boosters. There are no entries at all between 1964 and 1976—his fifties and early sixties. Hastily compressed in the small space at the top and bottom of the card, and written (like most of the other entries) in his own hand, is some detail about the fitting of a pacemaker (11.4.88) and about severe stomach pain (10.10.91). He has been a fit man, and there are only three entries of substance:

24.10.53 Diarrhoea, nausea and colic. PMA: SG age 8. Recurrent tonsillitis, Ts and As age 22.

9.6.64 Ruptured Tendon Achilles (L)

?.?.83 Ac Glaucoma. Bilaltl irridectomy

The last presumably refers to an eye problem, or operation, but did he ever tell me about it? What does PMA stand for in the first entry? Previous Medical Account? Ts and As must mean the removal of tonsils (and adenoids?) at twenty-two, an operation which, having endured or benefited from himself, he later inflicted on me and my sister. But what is SG? And why is there no record of the operation to relieve pain in his wrists? Here is the biography of his body, but so abbreviated and random I can find no way to connect it with him.

It's only the Achilles tendon rupture I can recall. One Whitsun holiday he had gone swimming at Airedale baths with my sister, then twelve, and had been teaching her how to dive. The previous year, I had been his hopeless pupil ('Don't keep bringing your knees down. What are you so afraid of?'), and now it was my sister's turn to be put through the hoop. He took her to the deep end to show how it was done. Running, leaping, then coming down heavily on the end of the board (and he was heavy then for a man of five foot eight: twelve and a half stone), he had snapped the tendon as he rose in the air, landed in the water with a flapping ankle, and had to be lifted from the pool. He realized what he'd done, but got himself home, strapped up the ankle and drove my sister the hundred miles back to her school in Windermere (less use of the clutch than usual?). Next day he saw the surgeon, who confirmed the rupture and kept him in hospital. It became family lore that this was what you got for showing off: three months in plaster, or worse. I wondered whether there hadn't been some young women in the pool other than my sister he was trying to impress—maybe that had been his Achilles heel.

Apart from some complaints about the itchiness of the cast,

he made a joke of it all—the doctor coming home in plaster
not from some chic Alpine skiing trip but from the local baths.
But jokes within the family were one thing; wearing his
indignity in front of patients was another. Far from reacting as
we expected—business as usual, a chauffeur wangled from
somewhere to get him out on his visiting rounds—he refused
to go to surgery in a wheelchair. It was an odd period, a long
six weeks: while he languished morosely at home, the other
two GPs in the practice (one of them my mother) had to cover
for him. 'Do you really need to go to Cawder Ghyll quite so
much?' he'd ask when she came back from the local maternity
hospital: guilty at the extra surgeries she had to take, he
somehow expected the pre- and post natal work she normally
did to fade away, for babies to have the decency to stop being
born for a bit. In the end, the third partner began to grumble: if
my father was so wheelchair-bound, how come he was still
drinking at the Cross Keys every night? The answer was that
my mother, bullied into it, drove him there—unloading him
from and reloading him into his wheelchair. But even her
patience was wearing thin: people were beginning to notice
what his wheelchair did and didn't allow him to do. A few days
later my father resumed surgery, on crutches.

By the time we went on holiday that August, he had
recovered his old spark. Friends had lent us a caravan on the
west coast of Scotland, and he was desperate not to sit it out
while the rest of us went shrimp-catching and flounder-
spearing. Fishermen's waders would not accommodate the
plaster cast; he used an empty plastic fertilizer bag instead, tying
the top with string so he could wade out up to his thighs. It
worked for a couple of days, until, inevitably, water penetrated
the bag and the cast began to loosen and break. He had to go
to the local hospital and get it reset. He came back, not shamefaced and reproached for having been so irresponsible, but

triumphantly carrying the old cast, signed by most of the hospital staff.

I put his medical history back on the desk, and start opening drawers. A diary from 1940 (his spell as houseman in Charing Cross Hospital). A newspaper cutting from 1942 ('CITY DOCTOR GOES ON MERCY TRIP . . . A Manchester RAF medical officer was among the crew of a Coastal Command Aircraft which saved the life of a Portuguese boy dangerously ill with Tetanus on one of the Atlantic islands of the Azores. Flight-Lieutenant A B Morrison answered an SOS call and delivered a supply of serum to 11-year-old . . . '). A programme for the Duke of York's Theatre, October 1946, to see E. Vivian Tidmarsh's farcical comedy *Is Your Honeymoon Really Necessary?* (it was his honeymoon). A menu for the Annual British Medical Association Dinner at the Swan Royal, Clitheroe, 1948 (shrimp cocktail, roast rib of English beef, assorted cheeses with celery, the toast to His Majesty the King). A ticket for the Colne Golf Club dance, 1949. The official racecard for the Pendle Forest and Craven Harriers Point-to-Point Steeple-chase, April 1955 (winners marked in pencil). A diary record of our first family holiday abroad, Majorca, 1961 (what bought, what drunk, where visited, rows over sun-loungers on the terrace: 'Fat Jew tried to pinch one we'd reserved'). Four torn-off cinema stubs (it must have been *South Pacific*, the only film we saw together as a family, my mother's idea, but my father in his cock-eyed element: 'A hundred and one pounds of fun/ That's my little honey-bun'). A ticket to the stock car races, Bellevue Stadium, Manchester, 8 October 1963 (my birthday, one of his magical mystery treats). A receipt for the Regent Palace Hotel, 29 July–1 Aug 1966 (the World Cup Final: we were standing down by the Russian linesman when he gave *that goal*, and left thinking the final score was 3–2 because the Germans didn't kick off again, joined the celebrations afterwards and heard the horns hooting all night in Piccadilly Circus). Another hotel receipt, for a week at the Cairngorm Hotel, Aviemore, 1969, cost forty-seven pounds, twelve shillings and threepence (our first shot at skiing, a holiday I'd buggered up for him by being confined to bed, my leg swollen from some insect bite).

I shut the drawer again. Every lunch and dinner, every theatre and sports outing, even the hotels where we stayed in the year of UCCA and my efforts to get a university place (he insisted on driving me to the interviews, of course, would have sat in on them if he could), nothing has been chucked, nothing let go of. I try another drawer, and another: cigarette lighters; leather watch-straps; a magnifying glass; Remembrance Day poppies; unsigned, cheeky-suggestive valentine cards (he to my mother, she or someone else to him, who could say: he always asked us not to sign greetings cards within the family, so they could be reused); a green plastic dagger with 'Dettol' written on it, his pharmaceutical freebie letter-opener. I shut the drawers again and close my eyes, and try to say their contents back to myself, like that memory game when a tray is put in front of you, then whisked away. And the objects I can recall all belong to the time before I was born. I hang on to them in a kind of desperation, as if, suddenly, all that I never had is lost and gone—a myth of having missed the best years by a breath: my parents first meeting each other; the war, and the strange numbness after the war; their marriage; their first and only practice. I close my eyes and try to see through the mist, the myth. But no picture comes into my head except a man at his desk under a venetian blind, a man in a forties suit holding an HB pencil, a man trying to sketch something—a design for what? a valentine? a menu? the first National Health Card?— but drawing a blank, and finally screwing the paper up: 'No good. Try again.'

★

At three I take his car out, pulling on the pair of leather gloves he's left on the passenger seat. I drive towards Elslack Moor, which I can see ahead fighting clear of the roak. I take the right fork in Elslack village and wind up the steep hill, over the beck, past the farm where the sheepdog used to run out and chase the car, up to the fir plantation where my father and I once found a magical object made of metal and canvas with a piece of withered rubber and a tag: a weather balloon (we had to complete and send back the tag), but to me, aged seven, a miracle.

I stop the car and walk to the summit, the white concrete cairn. The mist has wiped out the valleys below and I can hear only the tug and chomp of grazing sheep. My father used to say the places up here got their names from the time that Charles the First, or was it Cromwell, crossed the Pennines, en route to one of the great Civil War battles, Preston or Marston Moor. 'Hereby I pitch my tent' became Earby. 'Lo, there's a dale' became Lothersdale. 'What's yon foul ridge?' became Foulridge. I'd not believed him—as if the King or Lord Protector had had a scribe diligently at elbow to rename the kingdom—but never mind: *he* had told me, that's the only history that matters.

I walk back to the car. A Range Rover crashes across the cattle grid. There'd been a time when a drive out on the tops would be a long stop-start process through the sheep-dividing gates of various hill farms, my sister and I taking it in turns to get out and swing the five-barred gates open while the car passed through. You never got traffic in those days; you *were* the traffic. Now this is a busy road, the scenic cut-through from Colne to Keighley. I drive on a bit, then park again at the viewpoint the council has created above Earby. How different had it been when my parents arrived in 1946? There must have been half a dozen mill chimneys then, not just the one. The houses would all have been in that dark cobbled centre of terraces, not sprawling off in estates towards Sough and Barnoldswick. There would have been the wooden sleepers and iron flash of a railway line, whereas now there's only the white limestone underlay and (hapless, capless) two pillars where a bridge once stood. There would have been haber-dashers and ironmongers, not Chinese take-aways and video rentals. There would have been more smoke, more fields, less noise, fewer cars.

But the huddle of streets round the surprising green clear-ance of the cricket ground is little altered. And I can see our old house, the Crossings, where the main road, the A56, meets the Colne–Skipton railway line. There was a song when we lived there, 'The Train Runs Right through the Middle of the House', which seemed to have been composed especially for us. It wasn't a good place for patients to come with migraines, but until the practice moved to Water Street, in the fifties, they had no choice: surgery was held in the side of our house. I could remember a roll-top desk, antiseptic smells, a leather-covered bench in the waiting-room, silent, head-down, pale-faced visitors. The trains were an hourly nuisance. My mother's weighing-scales vibrated. My father gripped his syringe tightly. I was once found standing in the middle of the tracks.

What had he felt about Earby in his first years? He couldn't pretend to like the place much, the last and least of an eastward sprawl of mill-towns. He'd said during the war that, when it was over, he'd never want to stray more than fifty miles from his home, Manchester. Once out of the RAF, he'd begun by looking for something in Cheshire, nearer his parents. But the money his father had lent him to get started wasn't enough, could secure only this dead-end practice. There were con-solations. He loved the Dales. He wanted to be topdoc, number one GP, and succeeded in wooing patients from the other two local practices. He was still young, just over thirty, when the National Health Service began in 1948, and—though a Tory voter most of his life—was in many ways a model NHS pioneer, receptive to new ideas, with a woman partner, and glad that he no longer had to chase up patients for the two and six or four and six or whatever it was they owed him. In the sixties he flirted briefly with emigration to Canada or Australia, and with lusher practices in North Yorkshire, but in the end he stayed put until he retired—for thirty-five years, decade after decade of inexorable routine: surgery at eight-thirty, visits from twelve till two, a quick pint, home for a sandwich, zizz and cup of tea, surgery again from four-thirty till seven-thirty, another visit or two squeezed in on either side.

I've often wondered what kind of doctor he was. 'One of the most irascible buggers I'd ever come across,' was how one patient had described his first impressions, adding: 'It didn't take me long to realize my mistake.' But perhaps those first impressions were right. My father could be brusque and bad-tempered. He didn't go in for kind words and placebos. 'Fresh air and exercise' was to him the greatest cure for everything, and though by the end he handed out pills as freely as the next doctor I sometimes thought he'd have been happier in an older world of quack medicine and home-made cures. 'Give them drugs and they'll be better in a week,' he'd say, 'give them nothing and it'll be seven days.' I knew how unscientific he could be: masturbation was bad, he warned me when I was a teenager, 'because it weakens the organ for adult life.' He had his passions, notably diet: blaming himself for his father's coronary (if only he hadn't let him get so overweight), he cut down his own weight (from twelve and a half stones to eleven) and drew up a diet sheet for his patients. But what a diet sheet: 'YOU MUST NOT EAT bread, cakes, pastry, biscuits, butter, margarine, cream, fatty meats, sugar, jam, chocolate or potatoes,' it ran. 'YOU CAN EAT, in small amounts, green vegetables, lettuce, fresh fruit, fish, chicken and lean meat. ALWAYS get up still a bit hungry after each meal, and REMEMBER that if you eat enough of anything, grass even, you get fat—look at cows. AND REMEMBER: NO FAT PEOPLE CAME OUT OF BELSEN.' Earby and Barnoldswick had quite a few Polish refugees. We ourselves had an Austrian Jew for a housekeeper. He was lucky, perhaps, that no one passed his diet on to the local paper.

My father hadn't the temperament to be anything other than this kind of offensively no-nonsense doctor, though my mother—who worked less full-time in the surgery than he did, but to whom many patients, especially women, preferred to come—always justified his blunt manner by saying that it was what your average Earby patient needed: he didn't talk down to them, didn't dissemble, didn't muck about. And his toughness didn't run very deep: there was vulnerability and cack-handedness, too. One night he was called to deal with a drunk and violent man and decided that he couldn't sedate him by conventional means (impossible to get the needle in) and would have to knock him out instead: 'I went for a right hook rather than a jab.' The man was mildly shocked by the blow to his chin, calmed down and quietly went off to bed. My father had to go to hospital, having broken his little finger.

I peer down on the dimming lights of Earby and try to remember the last time I saw him in action. Only this morning, on his desk, I'd seen the chart he had with the names of his 'chronic' patients, fifty or sixty or more. Since retirement he's had a ritual of going to see them around Christmas, and of recording the date of every visit. The names of the deceased, marker-penned through in yellow, now outnumber those alive. This is going to be the first year he's not paid his Christmas visit. So maybe his last time as a doctor was five months ago, on holiday with me in Suffolk. A girl came off her bike outside our gate, a fat, piggy-pink twelve-year-old moaning and bleeding all over the road. I was worried about moving her, but he dragged her on to the lawn and pushed her hair back, trying to find where the blood was coming from. I ran inside for cotton wool, ran back, went in again to ring her parents. By the time I got back he'd washed the blood from her and was dabbing iodine on her face and legs—the iodine left ugly yellow stains, uglier than wounds. Her parents came and took her to hospital, 'for an X-ray, just in case'. A Thank You card came next day. My father was elated to have been useful again, to have helped and healed. But I kept thinking of those yellow stains and imagined the doctor in Casualty saying, as they brought her in: 'God, iodine, we don't use that on face-wounds any more. Who the hell's done this to her?'

Chastened, afraid, it's tempting for me to melt all his contradictions into a stream of hagiography. But I know the contradictions are there: the unsnobbish protector and defender of 'ordinary decent folk' had his big house, his Merc, his live-in maid, and was acutely aware of his social status; the sentimental family man could be a bully and tyrant; the open-hearted extrovert had a trove of secrets and hang-ups.

I drive down the hill past his old surgery in Water Street, the stream running fiercely under the stone footbridge that links the terraced houses to the street. When I get back to the house around five—the moon pouring in with a new child in its arms, grief coming through like a tooth—I find my mother still sitting as I'd left her, nothing and everything the same.

Carwash

I'M IN BED, avoiding my father. I know he has jobs lined up for me, because it's Sunday, and everywhere's closed on Sunday, and he's keen on us doing things together and being 'useful'. I hate being useful. Once I used to escape to church, to the choir—a chance to dress up in a white cotton surplice and hairy black cassock, a way of meeting the other three boys in the village. But now that I've stopped believing in God, now that I'm running away from the holy family, my one escape is the football I play on Sunday afternoons. Rain flusters against my bedroom window. I worry that today's match, against Bradley, will be called off. I close my eyes and imagine water gathering in the mud-brown stud-holes of Barnoldswick's recreation field. Please God, let it stop raining.

I have another worry, that my father will want to come and watch me, which embarrasses me, because he's a doctor, not like other boys' fathers, and with a posh car, a black Mercedes, which I don't want them to see. Luckily, he's not much interested in football. *His* sports as a boy were rugby, squash and tennis: 'Good eye for a ball I had. You have it, too. You should try rugby or tennis as well.' I did try tennis once, but he beat and barracked me so heavily I have not tried it again. Now that he's fifty, he is trying other sports, but he's not had much success. Yachting in Abersoch, he couldn't get the hang of tacking; the wind died on us, and we had to be towed back by a kid with an outboard (the car we'd left on the beach was about to disappear under the high tide). Riding in Anglesey, he lost a stirrup while galloping along the beach and for a mile or more clung on to the horse by its neck; friends hootingly observed it from a hotel balcony; he came back pale but grinning: 'Destry rides again.' He's fond of telling me to stick to ball games, and I want to tell him to do the same.

The rain eases at the window. It is eleven o'clock. I plan to stay here, reading Kerouac or Salinger or Mailer, until my ritualistic pre-match lunch of steak and chips. But now here's my father, pushing straight in, hoping to catch me up to no good.

'Come on, nose out of that book, up. I'll give you five minutes to get some old clothes on, I need some help washing the car.'

'I've a match later.'

'So? Plenty of time till then.'

'But it's cold.'

'Up. Half an hour it'll take, that's all. You've got to learn how to wash cars. You'll be starting to drive next year. Come on, up.'

I put my clothes on, wishing it were spring, when the job I help my father with is not car-washing but mowing the lawn. Mowing is a drag too, most of it—the sloping front lawn, the two raised back ones—but I love cutting the grass verges out by the road (a chance to look at girls in passing cars, and for them to look at me), and I love the moment when I turn the engine off and run my fingers through my hair—the mower's vibrations soften my hands and make my hair feel silky-sensual, like a shampoo advert.

It's freezing up by the garage. There is a cobbled area in front of the old barn, and this is where my father's car is standing, his black Mercedes, his red-and-white Metropolitan, his drop-head Triumph Vitesse, his maroon Alvis, or whatever model currently meets his requirements of being open and sporty. Car-washing, he thinks, is a DIY task: coin-in-the-slot alternatives have begun to spring up, with their woolly roller-bales and double row of changing-room showers, but he'll have no truck with them. Car-washing is as integral a part of his Sunday as a cooked breakfast or the blazer and cravat worn to the pub. It's more than a conforming, middle-class anality. Car-washing to him is part of learning about cars, a process he's inducted me in since I was eight, when he put a moped engine in the back of my old pedal car and taught me to drive, a process continued more recently, in his car, on the Polish airfield near Pwllheli, the beach at Black Rock Sands, the skid patch at Criccieth, and anywhere else you don't need a driving licence. But car-washing is about something else, too: he wants his cars to look clean and respectable because he thinks that makes them less *noticeable*, less *criminal*, when he's speeding, as he usually is. Police-evasion is high-priority with us: he has had a second mirror installed, on the left of the windscreen, so that passenger as well as driver can keep a look-out for patrol cars behind. When my mother isn't his front-seat passenger, my sister or I play security man for him. He did the driving, and I did the mirror, during his greatest ever journey—when he covered the 181 miles to North Wales (no motorways, B-roads mainly) in 180 minutes. He prefers dawn runs like that because the roads are clear, and he can drive at eighty in built-up areas. Once he had to speed off down narrow side-streets in Rawtenstall to lose a chasing police car; another time he *was* stopped, but sorry-sirred the squad car constable, let drop the fact of his profession, and got off with a warning. He has never been fined, never had his licence endorsed. He puts this down to the self-effacing cleanness of his cars.

I stand watching him as he makes sure the car doors and windows are properly closed: 'Tight, mind: water can get through the tiniest crack.' He hands me the hose-pipe, whose floppy octogenarian pee I dangle vaguely over the bonnet.

'No, not like that—it's kinked under your foot, look. That's better. Now put your thumb over the end.'

I do this, but the spray is erratic, hissing off over the car roof one moment and down inside my wellingtons the next. Gradually, as my thumb turns to ice, I begin to control it better, until there's a steady forked tongue of spray, which spitters on the bonnet and boot simultaneously, but omits the whole side of the car. I ease my thumb back a bit more, and at last I've got the full, solid eight-pints-in-the-pub-gents power-stream my father's been looking for.

'That's it. There's only one right way to wash a car.'

'I know, Dad.'

'Hose it first. Start at the top . . . '

'Then work down . . . I know.'

'Bonnet, sides and hub-caps last of all.'

The two dishcloths are in a red bucket of hot soapy water. I plunge my chapped hands in, and keep them there as long as I can, making a great ceremony of squeezing and re-squeezing the cloth. My father is enjoying himself—triumphant at forcing me from my warm bed, absorbed in a practical task, glad of the company and someone to boss around. We work together, swishing the warm cloths, taking it in turns with the hose, going over the little mud-streaks we've missed. My ears ache in the December wind, my duffel coat is sodden from the misdirected hose, my toes in the damp wellingtons have gone missing. My father, in his thin overalls, is happy.

Out on the road there's a screeching of brakes, and my

father says: 'Christ. They still can't negotiate that corner.' The 'corner' is a T-junction just beyond our driveway. Until the council improved it, every other Sunday seemed to bring an accident. I remember one lunchtime two years ago, a loud bang and chandelier-fall of glass, my father's knife and fork left on the edge of his plate in a smear of horseradish as he ran down the drive with his bag. I skipped pudding and peered over the wall where bushes hid me. The motorcyclist under the lorry was white-faced, not moving and half-hidden by the wheel. My father crouched over him in the rain. An ambulance came, and more people crouched by the lorry's grille. When the fire engine arrived I went back in. I couldn't imagine how they'd get the motorcyclist free. Lately there have been no accidents, but as we swish and spray my father recalls some of the worst he has had to attend: the young lovers hit by the Nelson–Skipton train at an open level crossing ('Just bits—couldn't identify them'); the lad in a van who braked too hard and was decapitated by the metal extension ladder he'd propped in the back; the girl run over by the school bus ('at a pedestrian crossing—criminal'); the woman found dead on the moors, MURDER headlines in the paper until her boyfriend went to the police weeks later ('choked to death—when you're older I'll tell you what happened'). The talk is ghoulish but my father's tones are comforting. By talking about accidents he hopes to ward them off, perhaps—or to interest me in his work.

'So what are you going to study in the sixth form do you think?'

'Oh, you know—I seem to be best at English and languages. Something like that.'

'And what career would that lead to?'

'Teaching, I suppose. Or journalism, maybe.'

'Journalism? That usually means London. The *Yorkshire Post*'s not a bad paper, though.'

'Or law.'

'A profession, that's the thing to aim at.'

'Yes, Dad.'

'But if you do sciences in the sixth form,' he says, bending over the silver platter of the hub-cap, 'surely you'd have more choice of career. Even if you're not a genius at science, and it's a bit of a chore for two years, at least you can read medicine later on.'

'I know, Dad.'

'And medicine is different, not a science exactly, more practical—you'd enjoy it.'

'I know, you've said.'

'I want you to do what you want to do, but Mummy and I have built up this practice, and I don't suppose Gill is likely to be a doctor, and if you took over, a son taking over from his father, and by then you'd be married probably, and you could live nearby with your wife and children, that would be marvellous, all of us together.'

'Hum.'

'Think about it.'

I'm on the hub-caps now, feeling through the cloth the grains of muck that have sploshed and stuck there from puddles and ditches and gritted roads. I scrub hard to be rid of them, the old mud-stains and scratches, until the circles of chrome shine in their dark rubber like full moons.

'The Riviera, look,' my father says, as the sun breaks through the clouds and a sheen comes off the bodywork. I pick up the hose again from where it's bleeding into the metal drain, and aim it noisily at the wheels. I empty the bucket's foamy black liquid, fill it with cold water from the stable tap, and pick up the chamois wash-leather. It is a khaki colour, hard and stiff and fossilized, like a small plaice: it makes me think of a poem we've been reading at school this week, Auden's 'Miss Gee'. I dip it in the bucket, where it changes its nature, softens, plumps out. I hand it to my father, who wrings its neck.

'Clean as a whistle,' he says, as he finishes wiping and the last yelps die on the windscreen. 'There's a fault on the brake-light I need to fettle, but you go in and warm up if you want.'

'I wouldn't mind.'

'Remember what I said. Not a bad life, being a doctor. There'd be a practice all waiting—a son taking over from his father, people respect that. Think on.'

Johnson's Baby Powder

THERE IS A low point that comes when you've been sitting by a sickbed—around six, say, after the light has gone, about the time you pour yourself the first anaesthetizing short. My father has been asleep since Dr May left this morning, his head back on the pillow, his mouth wide open so that you can see (I've never noticed before) the uneven run of his bottom teeth. Sitting on the dressing-table stool next to my mother, both of us with Glenfiddichs, I feel suddenly, clearly, that he will not wake again. The dog skitters into the room and fusses round our feet, his coat—through my glass—the colour of whisky. 'Poor little Nikki, you don't understand,' says my mother. 'You don't know what day it is. You don't know what's happening up here.'

For the last few days, my father, whenever he sits on the edge of the bed and Nikki comes running, has had to spread his hands out in front of him (as if warming them on the fire) to stop the dog jumping into his naked lap, and the dog has slunk away, not used to such rejection. But his animal bewilderment isn't so different from our own informed incomprehension. A tear falls on my shoe, another on to the carpet between my feet. I keep my head down, not wanting my mother to see, but she passes me some paper tissues and says, not unkindly: 'Better do your crying alone.'

Is it this that wakes my father? Suddenly he is there again, alert, wanting a pee, and walks unaided to the bathroom. 'Walk' is maybe not the word. It is like swimming in some new element, performing some previously unperformed task. There's been a National Electricity advertisement on television lately, in which a gang of pylons shuffle into life and stride stiff-jointedly across the countryside; his walk is like this. Yet his penis is gratifyingly large, not the shrivelled miniature rose, and he pees, a triumph. Back in bed, he leans towards the glass of iced water I'm holding for him and cups his hands shakily round the glass, trying to get his lip over the top of the straw. As he drinks, the fingers of my right hand, cooled by the glass, touch his left nipple, which hardens a little—a bright pink pearl, not the slack, down-tilting brown teat of earlier. The folds of skin under his breasts are like some fancy rucked curtain, parted at the middle. Across his chest, stomach, back, shoulders is the familiar fallout of birthmarks and moles.

For the next hour he slips in and out of sleep. My sister arrives, briefed now that we won't have him much longer, and whenever he closes his eyes and seems to fade away we bring him back him with some question, like parents coming in late from a party and—drunk, elated, sentimental—waking their baby for a play. I tell him what's been on the news: a train crash in the Severn Tunnel, not any dead; the latest about Robert Maxwell's missing millions, the financial mess his sons have inherited; fighting in Dubrovnik. He shakes his head in a what's-the-world-coming-to way. I tell him some of the football results, and he makes me fetch his pools coupon from his desk. He has done the pools without success for forty years, the same complicated perm every week. I can find no record of it among the mass of paper, so he dictates it from memory:

'One, the cross is in column E, three D, four F, six A, seven B, seven C, nine F,' and so on up into the fifties. It's a slow process, in and out of consciousness, but when I later turn up his master copy and check his memory against it I find it's almost faultless. This is the poignant thing: his body is clanking into a grassed-over siding, but his mind is humming along perfectly. When I tell him that *Match of the Day* is on, Bolton v. Blackpool in the FA Cup second round, two great old teams now in lower divisions, he says:

'Grandpa bought one of his cars in Blackpool, an Austin, FX 709, a Blackpool number-plate. And he was once going to a football match at Bolton, his team, a big all-ticket job against Blackpool, and the queue of cars was terrible, so he said "Bugger this" and drove past them up the outside. When he got to the front, the steward flagged him down, angry-looking, thinking he was queue-jumping, then saw his Blackpool number-plate and waved him straight into the visitors' car park, the Blackpool supporters' end.'

'So that's where you got the habit of jumping queues,' says Gill.

'What about your own cars?' I ask, stilted as a fifties BBC interviewer. 'There was some story, wasn't there?'

'Which one do you mean? There was my little Austin, my first car, and I was so proud of it, but I had this problem with the handbrake cable. I put some oil on, but the oil didn't seem to be going down the cable tube, so I thought if the engine turned over and I had a short run out on the main road that might help, but I was so busy looking down at the cable I drove into a lamppost.'

'And didn't you crash into some railings in Manchester once?'

'I was trying to reverse into a tight space and I couldn't see, so I leant across to open the passenger door to get a better view, and I knocked the car into third gear and it shot forward across the road up on to the pavement and against some coping stones supporting railings. There were girls working in an office basement there, and masonry came pouring down through their window, and they all came out to see what had happened. I was about twenty. They were sniggering at me in my blazer and tie. I had to ring Grandpa to help get me out and tow me home. I felt a prize fathead.'

'At least it wasn't like blowing up the tram in Bolton,' says my sister, coaxingly, prompting him to embark on another old story, about how he and two schoolfriends raided the chemistry lab and laid some explosive they'd mixed on the tramlines in Bolton. We know the tale by heart—the loud bang, the tram-driver scratching his head, the traffic brought to a standstill, the pranksters sneaking away unnoticed. To hear him tell it is comforting—for a moment, death seems to have receded. But then again, not: for us to cajole him into telling stories which we've spent most of our lives being bored or exasperated by is a sign of how desperate we've become, how little we believe we'll ever hear them—or him—again. It's like the ornaments or pictures on the wall I've always hated, the lolling dogs, cutesy goose-girls and naff souvenirs, suddenly precious now. We don't want different stories; we want the same stories. And it doesn't matter what he says, only that he says something: now that everything is a last thing, even the most banal utterance is depth-charged.

In the kitchen, my cousin Kela has arrived from Ormskirk. She has been told not to, but she has come: 'This is family. He thinks he can get away without seeing me, but he's bloody well not going to, the pet.'

We've always called her Kela, but her real name is Mikela,

after her father, Michael, who went missing over France two weeks before she was born. Along with Ronnie Astle, Mike Thwaites had been my father's best friend: the three of them were schoolmates, played the same games, mucked about in the same cars, went into the RAF together. My father's sister Mary had married Mike in 1940; after his death, after Kela's birth, after the war, she married Ronnie, and they had three more children of their own, Richard, Edward and Jane. We used to spend every Christmas with them, Yorkshire one year, their house near Manchester the next. Kela, the odd one out, a Thwaites rather than an Astle, has always cherished my father as a lost link with her father, who is a man she never knew, a ghost, a god, an RAF hero. She sits half an hour with my father, then is back in the kitchen with her poor, dry, eczema-flaky skin, her fags, her glass of wine, her laughter, her unfailing cosiness. Since Auntie Mary died of cancer ten years ago, Kela, herself nearly fifty now, has appointed herself chief Holder Together of the Family. Despite the official protests, we're glad she is here. She makes it easier for us to indulge ourselves, to harp on the past, though the past we harp on is a score of death not of life.

'Dear old Uncle Arthur,' Kela says. 'Hanging on, just like Mummy did.'

'Does cancer run in families?' I ask.

'You mean, is it genetic?' my mother says. 'Or does a certain sort of person . . . I don't know, love. Your father is hardly the repressed sort. Nor was Mary. And they had very different personalities.'

'Mummy had a year after they found the primary,' says Kela. 'She was walking round with a colostomy bag.'

'And she didn't deny it like Dad?'

'At first she did. But once the secondaries were found she was talking openly about dying. She wasn't afraid of death itself—only of choking or the horrible pain there might be. And then, the love, she left these notes about the house for us, in drawers and cupboards, which we kept finding afterwards: "Families need each other," "Keep seeing one another after I'm not here," "No worries about me where I've gone."'

'And it wasn't a horrible death?'

'No, we were all there, and chatting not long before. Then a few minutes before she died she said, "I can't find Michael."'

'My brother Patrick was a bit like that,' says my mother. 'The last thing he said was: "There's my mother at the end of the bed."'

Kela drains her wine glass and lights another cigarette.

'At least Mummy died peacefully,' she says.

'Granny, too,' says my mother, rehearsing the old details of her mother-in-law's death. 'Fine until she was eighty-six. Then she began to have trouble with her hands, they became twisted and useless, and she couldn't play the piano any more. One morning she said: I'm fed up, I want to die. Later that afternoon she was screaming out with pain—I gave her some pethidine, only a small dose, but she never recovered consciousness.'

'You mean you eased her on her way,' I say.

'No, she was eighty-seven, with an abdominal infarct—I was saving her from pain. I did the same for my brother Patrick. He was in a hospital run by nuns, last stages of cancer, and I was sitting there, and he was in such agony because they were mingy with the morphine, the dose they gave was about as strong as a Smartie. So I went to the sister and said: could he have an extra dose? He died later that night. It's a mercy, when you're never going to recover anyway.'

I open another bottle of wine. We make up a bed for Kela. There are fronds and crab-claws of frost on the window.

★

I dream I'm at the office. Reception call up: 'A gentleman to see you—says he has an appointment.'

'Tell him I'll be down.'

I'm expecting no one, I realize, and up to my eyes: I have widows to turn, kill fees to negotiate, a paper to put to bed. I decide to make him wait. Soon I relent and go down.

'He was sitting over there. Must have gone.'

'What was his name?'

'Didn't say.'

'What did he look like?'

'Your size. Thinning hair.'

'What age?'

'Old enough to be your father.'

I rush out into City Road. No sign. I search the Underground. No one. I walk in circles round the graveyard in Bunhill Fields. Nothing.

Sunday morning, and I can hear my father's voice as I wake. He has just had my mother make him a second breakfast: the spoonful of Complan wasn't enough, he wanted a quarter cup of cornflakes too. Now he feels in need of a shower, and I fit a new light-bulb in the cubicle for him as he soft-shouts the instructions from the bed: 'Twist the old light-bulb in and leftwards to release it. Got it? Right, now push the new one in and rightwards to insert it.' Is it that he assumes I still don't know how to change a light-bulb? Or that his is the one infallible method, the beautiful simplicity of which he thinks the rest of the world hasn't yet cottoned on to? I take heart from my irritation: he must be feeling better.

Not that he can be, much. I watch him stagger to the shower, loose skin flapping like an elephant's. His chest looks as if someone has ploughed across it, deep furrows between the three huge top ribs. His pacemaker, once buried in the fat of his chest, now stands proud, like a parcel on a doormat; I can even see the contact points, top right, where the two wires come into it. After the shower, which he takes leaning with one hand against the wall, he lies on the bed and asks my mother to powder his bottom—Johnson's Baby Powder, the sweet whiff of it—'and maybe the balls, too, they get trapped.' She puffets out the white powder from the big phallic container, then smears its strange silkiness across him, under him. Johnson's Baby Powder: the Johnson's factory is nearby, in Gargrave; he was powdered as a child with it, he saw his children powdered, now he is being powdered for death. My mother's hand is under his sac, then she kisses his forehead and leaves the room quickly, tears behind her glasses.

By the time Richard and Edward arrive an hour later, he's sitting in his chair by the fire, head bowed, shirt open, modesty hankie in position. They had expected, from our phone call yesterday, a man close to death, but the one in the chair who lifts his head is comparatively sparky. Richard has come from Manchester, Edward all the way from London, though both pretend they just happened to be passing: they don't want him to think there's anything unusual about their being here, don't want to alarm him. I feel guilty, as if we've got them here under false pretences: there's no knowing, he might still be alive in three months. This is the rollercoaster of terminal illness, and already I can hear a little voice in me starting up that resents his tenacity, his ability to pull himself back up off the floor, that whispers, beneath the spoken pieties: *Just die, will you.* Even his cheeriness is needling. 'It's no fun having a major operation,' he says, adding: 'But there's a long way to go yet.' He drifts off—until we start talking about getting Kela's car started in the heavy frost, and he wakes to issue instructions about a battery charger and jump leads.

Later, I wheedle my cousins to the pub. The fields crunch under our feet like cereal flakes, whiteness all the way to heaven. The double canal bridge at East Marton looks at itself several times in the water. Just above it is the Cross Keys, one of my father's two locals, the pub he began going to when it was taken over by Hilly and Brian Thackeray, who became close friends. From the bar where we drink our bitter, I see a face I half-recognize, and which seems to half-recognize me. It's a rather sulky, broken, impatient face, which—as I sneak looks at it through my glass—pieces itself together as an old schoolfriend, Charles Torrance. One summer I'd gone on holiday with his family to Seahouses, in Northumberland, and played cricket all day every day on the long, white, windy beach. Another summer he worked with me behind the bar of a club on a caravan site in North Wales, before he ran into trouble for refusing to serve (an eighteen-year-old's mad moral fervour) a fat blonde woman known to be having an affair with the site plumber. I hadn't seen him for twenty years but here he was now, unmistakable in his red golf club sweater, the same odd mixture of priggishness and nerves.

'Charles,' I say, walking over.

'Blake—I thought it was you.'

We talk for a minute as his son bleep-bleeps away on his Game Boy. Charles too has moved away, lives in Sussex now, a solicitor, here for the weekend. He asks after my father, and I remember his, Tim, also a doctor, but grander, a consultant, dapper, with a striped blazer and tie, in his youth a county schoolboy cricketer. At my parents' New Year parties, Tim had usually been the one who opened the piano lid and began to play. And when my father pressed me to continue with piano lessons it was always Tim's example he cited ('Marvellous to have a musical gift'), success in this field meaning not a faultless performance in a concert-hall (my father had never in his life been to one of those: 'A lot of people paying a lot of money to see something that's meant to be heard: no thanks') but a drunken singsong round the joanna. To my father's chagrin, I soon gave up on the piano—and playing the drums later for a group called The Crofters was no compensation, since we performed just the once (coming second out of two in a Gargrave talent contest) and our one song was a plaintive tune which he mockingly christened 'The Camel Driver's Lament'. Often, though, watching *Top of the Pops*, he'd enthuse over the power of music to 'send people', and I knew he must have envied Tim his musical talent. He himself could only whistle, and then just a few bars of the one tune he knew: 'Put Another Nickel In'.

Sitting here listening to the jingles of the Game Boy, I remember other things about Tim: how he had taken to calling on my mother for a late-afternoon or early-evening drink, and how they'd talk in hushed voices in front of the wide living-room windows. In some ways they seemed more suited than my mother and father were: Tim was clever, and I suspected my mother of being cleverer, academically at least, than my father. Tim was chivalrous too, like something out of a Noel Coward play, and my mother, as a young woman, had evidently been used to chivalry (one summer I'd found on her shelves a privately printed book of poems by one Michael McKenna, with the poet's inscription: 'To my love Agnes, with all my heart'). Tim belonged to her lost world of love and music. He even had a romantic's self-destructive streak—a drink problem. Sometimes he'd stay on all evening and have to be driven home in his Rover, my father plonking him in the passenger seat and taking the wheel, my mother following behind in our car to get my father home again—the alcoholic's convoy. Tim had died of a liver complaint, much too young.

My mother had been one of the few people to visit him in hospital.

Now I'm sitting here with his son, sour-faced and tense as ever, and *his* son, more of a charmer like Tim. We talk with my cousins, over another pint, of the pressures of work and mortgages. We agree it's time we abandoned our complex, urban, high-pressure lives, and moved here to live simply in the Dales. And all of us know that none of us is going to do it.

Back home, Richard, Edward and Kela gone, my father asleep, my mother and I sit at the foot of the bed, drink and death strengthening the feeling that there need be no secrets now, that anything can be spoken.

'There must have been things you've missed, living with Dad,' I say.

'Like what?'

'Oh, I don't know—books, music, company.'

'Company! You must be joking—you know how sociable he is, always at the pub, always asking people back.'

'But your sort of company—dinner parties and so on.'

'Oh, he hates dinner parties—going to someone's, and then feeling you have to have them in return. We've never once held a dinner party. He's very unsure of himself, though he never lets on, and I think that's part of it: at a dinner table, if the talk turns to things he doesn't know about, he feels trapped —whereas in the pub he can always go and buy a drink and talk to someone else. He won't even play Trivial Pursuit in case he shows his ignorance. And he can be a real sod. I remember when we first moved to Earby, the Melwards, a nice couple, asked us to a concert. He wouldn't go, of course, but I did and enjoyed it, and we must have stopped off for a drink on the way home, but it wasn't late, only ten-thirty, so I asked them in for a coffee—and there he was opening the front door in his pyjamas and asking where we'd been: I could have died of shame. Naturally, they never asked me again after that.'

'He doesn't read either.'

'And doesn't go to plays or exhibitions, and uses the television to fall asleep to: I know. I sometimes feel sorry for him not reading. I feel guilty in bed, looking forward to the moment he says, "Well, goodnight, love," and is snoring, so I can turn the light back on. After all, Granny used to read, and Mary, and my mother, too—all day long.'

'Was that why you liked Tim?'

'Oh, Tim was so sad,' she says, 'so many talents, so wasted. It was an unhappy marriage—Cheryl was always *nice and disapproving.*'

'He was keen on you, wasn't he?'

'Yes, I suppose, but I wasn't the type for affairs and I wouldn't have wanted to hurt Cheryl. It was better left as it was, just drinks and chat.'

'But no one would have blamed you. It would have made you feel better, getting your own back on Dad.'

'For Beaty, you mean?'

'Yes.'

'But I don't think that was an affair, not physical. I think Dad just felt sorry for her. That was such an unhappy marriage, too.'

'So you knew all about Beaty and Dad?'

'Yes. He was very open. I suppose I behaved like a doormat, but I thought: if I just sit this out it will peter away. Which it did.'

'But it went on a long time.'

'Ten years. And it hurt, of course. But I couldn't ask him to leave. And I knew if I ever tried to leave with you and Gillian he'd come after me, wherever I was—he idolized you both.

111

And I couldn't have left you either. So I had to put up with it.'

'It surprises me he wasn't secretive about it; he was in other ways.'

'He told me once in the billiard room that it was possible to love two women. And he did—I was his first love, he said, and she was his second, but in a different way.'

'Not everyone would have stuck it.'

'I could never argue with your father—no one could. There was one holiday when he suddenly announced we must take Beaty and Josephine, too. I thought it was outrageous— we were staying at a friend's, it wasn't our place to be inviting others along to. But in the end, of course, he got his way.'

'I can remember her coming.'

'But I still think it wasn't sexual. Oh, I suppose after Gillian I got post natal depression and wasn't much fun to be with. And she had the golf club and loved to drink. He started taking her out once a week. It became a ritual—Monday nights, giving her a good time, because things at her home were so miserable and Sam such a wet. Dad went to fetch her straight from surgery those evenings, never came home. I had to cover for him. I often wondered if you guessed when I said he'd gone to see J. J. Duckworth or to the Rotary Club. There was once he took her to a club in Blackburn, and met someone we knew—eventually that got back to me. And then his father died, and he hadn't seen much of him just before and he was *devastated*. And I suppose maybe Beaty offered him more sympathy than I did. Granny came to live with us, because Grandpa had said in a note that, if he died before her, the one thing he asked of Arthur and Mary was that Granny never spend a single night alone. So Dad moved her in and also insisted that I sleep in the same room—the back bedroom. Sometimes he'd come in at three, and I'd go through and ask, "Where have you been?" and he'd say, "Out." I discovered later he used to drive up on to the moors on his own and just sit there.'

'He told you that?'

'Yes.'

'I remember you packing your bags once.'

'Maybe. I went to stay with friends a couple of times. But I could never have left you.'

'And in the end it paid off.'

'Yes, it faded out.'

'And Josie isn't my half-sister?'

'No. How could you even think it?'

'I convinced myself there was a physical resemblance. And I remember him taking us to the maternity hospital to see her. Years later I thought I could see it all suddenly making sense.'

'He never takes any interest in Josie now, never even mentions her: if she'd been his surely he would have.'

'No, I see I was wrong.'

'Well, then . . . '

'And Uncle Sam put up with it all too, just like you.'

'Yes, I suppose he hated Dad's guts, but there wasn't much he could do.'

'And you've been happy since?'

'For the past twenty years your Dad and I have got on better than ever. He said to me, that long day we had before his operation: "We've been happy, pet, haven't we? I was a bastard to you sometimes, I know, but we were happy." All marriages have their difficulties. We got through ours in the end.'

Her eyes are red-rimmed as she tells me all this, though she doesn't cry and even if she did I wouldn't know the reason— for my father's approaching death, or for the freshened memories of what he'd done to her in his life.

The Man who Invented the
Outdoor Sleeping-Bag

THE SKY IS clear and my father is smiling. In public, at work, he smiles on principle: sociability demands it; a frown or deadpan look he deplores as 'ignorant' or 'pig-ignorant'. Today, though, just family, he's smiling because he's happy. He's sitting outside our newly-acquired second home, a caravan, or 'chalet' as we're taught to call it, perched on a sand-dune in Abersoch, North Wales—his favourite place, venue of his childhood holidays, source of all requirements for a happy life: sun, sand and sea. Over his shoulder is a bank of marram-grass and, beyond, white beach, a frill of breakers, two islands floating in the bay. He's smiling because it's warm—he has no shirt on, only a pair of shorts. He's smiling because he's working, cranking the wheel of an ancient sewing-machine, which whirrs and clicks under his hands. And he's smiling because these are the final touches to his latest invention, a sleeping-bag that will allow him to sleep in comfort outdoors.

Worldly rationalist though he was, or liked to think he was, my father had an eccentric side, which expressed itself every decade or so in A New Invention. He spoke often of the 'genius' of the man who invented Cat's-eyes for night driving, and he aspired to a similarly grand scientific breakthrough. His

114

first effort, or the first he thought worth approaching the patents office about, was the electric toothbrush anti-gunge protector. When he enthusiastically bought an electric toothbrush shortly after they were introduced in Britain, his one complaint was that the water and toothpaste tended to slide down the brush into the battery-operated base and to reduce efficiency. He designed a new sort of brush with a series of spiky protrusions which would deflect the gunge away from the base, and he sent off his design to the manufacturers. Disappointingly, they seemed to have felt that as well as deflecting gunge, the spiky protrusions would also tear into, perhaps even tear apart, the mouth and gums of the user—at any rate, my father received only a polite acknowledgment of his 'interesting proposal, which we have passed on to the relevant department.'

His Elsan Enhancer perhaps deserved a better fate. He had often complained, on having to use Elsans—non-flush toilets —on camp-sites or at large outdoor events, that the smell of other people's bodily waste was one thing, the sight of it another. Wouldn't the whole experience be more bearable if the Elsan contents, whether low in the well or (worse) rising towards the seat, could be concealed? He came up with the solution—a circular white disc, made of lavatory paper, but perhaps rather thicker in texture, to be dropped or lowered into the Elsan after use, thereby hiding the horror-show below. I expressed my concern that the white disc, even if people did take the trouble to use it, would sink out of sight or lose its whiteness. But he dismissed my reservations and wrote con-fidently to the manufacturers, expecting, I think, an enthusiastic response, a cheque, a consultative role to the Elsan Design Dept or even an honorary place on the board. He received no reply, not even to his second letter, and the Elsan Enhancer went the way of his other inventions, just as Elsans themselves (as he later vengefully liked to point out) became scarcer and scarcer in the age of flush-toilet affluence.

Chastened by these experiences, my father kept his next, and last, invention to himself.

Throughout my childhood he had been in the habit of sleeping outdoors whenever the weather was warm enough to permit it, and sometimes when it wasn't. He slept on the back lawn, outside the front porch, down the drive and (when I was grown up) on the roof terrace of my flat in Greenwich. But his favourite venue was the terrace of his chalet. Baden-Powellishly full of the joys of the alfresco kip—'Marvellous. Fresh air. Nothing between you and the sky. Can't beat it'—he seemed to spend more and more of each summer away from his bed. I worried what it signified, but my mother never complained of his habit, beyond a wry comment or two when clear night skies turned to rain by morning. *His* one complaint was that his sleeping-bag, which he would sleep in fully dressed on a camp-bed, always ended up damp and clammy, whatever: 'It's either rain or condensation. No bloody way round it.'

But finally he thought of a way. Suppose he were to place the sleeping-bag inside *another* sleeping-bag, made of plastic, like an envelope slipped inside a second, tougher envelope. He got hold of a reject roll of plastic from Armorides, the local factory, and cut it into two coffin-sized strips. Then he taught himself how to operate my mother's sewing-machine, a victory of will-power over instinct, since my father had not previously mastered, or shown signs of wanting to master, any domestic task he considered 'feminine'. He had never, to my knowledge, darned a sock, sewn on a button, boiled an egg, washed or ironed a shirt, swept the floor, cleaned the cooker or vacuumed the carpet. And it was only once he'd retired that, after a fashion, he attempted the washing-up: spurning the Fairy Liquid bottle, he'd hold items of cutlery or crockery one at a time under a trickling hot tap and scrub them shiny-clean with a nail-brush. But he did always insist on dressing crabs: no one else, he thought, could be trusted to remove the dead men's fingers. And now in his fifties he taught himself to sew.

His first sleeping-bag took some time to complete. But having succeeded, he decided he might as well make three more, 'for all the family', then another two, 'for when you have friends down . . . Pity to waste the plastic.' He was so pleased by what he saw he'd have gone on to make a seventh, but he had run out of material. I have a photograph of him grinning like a crazed scientist at the wheel of the sewing machine. The first time I made use of his invention, with him eagerly monitoring my reactions from the next camp-bed, must have been around the time the photograph was taken.

'What a spectacle,' he said as we lay in our outdoor sleeping-bags looking upwards into a night slashed and grazed by shooting stars, 'doesn't it make you feel small?'

It was a Saturday night, and for once, instead of the wind clinkety-clanking in the boat rigging like a Hare Krishna troupe, the air was silent, the sea calm as stone.

'Have you ever thought,' my father went on, 'that just as we are like tiny atoms in the universe, so the universe itself might be just a tiny atom in another universe? Or that each atom in your body might be a universe in a different dimension? Weird thought—sort of scares the shit out of you, space does.'

There were shrieks from the shoreline: someone larking about, a swim in the phosphorescence.

'When you look up there and think that the light from those stars set off hundreds of years ago, and then beyond them are the millions of stars you can't see except with a telescope, and they're thousands of light years away. We can't be the only intelligent life in the universe. It's a matter of making contact: if we keep sending signals from Jodrell Bank and so on, in different codes and languages, some day something will come back.'

Another shriek: salt water, a gentle swell, the surprising warmth of two bodies meeting . . .

'What do you think life can have been like at the start? You look up there and it's obvious the stars are different bits of the one thing that blew apart when time began. Imagine them rushing together again. Imagine reassembling that first planet or universe.'

'Reassembling?' I said, playing God's advocate. 'So it must have been assembled in the first place, someone invented it.'

A woman's cry, a man's guffaw.

'No, it just happened—primeval soup, a sudden spark, then, bang, time began. No one could have *made* all those stars.'

'Oh, I don't know,' I said, straining to catch the sound of someone, two people rather, in the sand below us. 'Think of all the frog-spawn that comes out of a single frog.'

'Oh, so you think someone *laid* the universe, like a bloody great bird laying an egg? And what's a shooting star supposed to be then? An egg falling out of the nest?'

We bickered on a bit about creation. Below us, the sighs and moans and sand-scuffles ebbed away, to be replaced by my father's immense snore—so immense I imagined it setting in motion a cosmic rhythm which would rock the stars backwards and forwards in unison. Across the bay, the lighthouse on St Tudwall's island flashed through the night, went out while I counted to twelve, then swung round into sight again, slicing up the darkness like a cake-knife. I shivered and wished I were man enough to be able to fall asleep, or, if not that, man enough to tell my father I'd had enough and was going in to my bed.

I woke at six, not only cold but damp. My father was awake already.

'All right, son?'

'Hum. My sleeping-bag feels wet.'

'Yes. When it's a clear night, there's condensation on the inside of the plastic as well as the outside—I suppose it's soaked through to your sleeping-bag as well.'

'So the outdoor sleeping-bag isn't working.'

'Course it is—it'd be much worse if you didn't have it. And on rainy nights you don't get condensation.'

'But on rainy nights you wouldn't want to sleep out.'

'Christ, you *have* got out of the wrong side of the bed, haven't you.'

'I'm still in it, Dad—and I'm soaked through.'

We squabbled some more. I told him I'd never use one of his sodding sleeping-bags again, but then did so later that summer, after a party with Carlsberg Special Brew, and in the company of two friends. He must have seen I was 'fresh' (his affirming, exculpatory word for the stale predictability of drunkenness), but was delighted to see his invention being put to the test and helped us assemble the camp-beds. I remember nothing after that but the sky spinning round and me hanging my head over the side of the camp-bed. He was furious next morning ('Can't hold your drink: I'm ashamed of you'), but at least with the outdoor sleeping-bag we were able to wipe the sick off and not leave a mark.

For the next ten years I hardly visited the Abersoch chalet. My father didn't use it as much, either, and by the late eighties it had gone into decline: paint was flaking on the shutters he'd made to protect the windows from winter tides; bits of roof had been torn off in the 1987 hurricane; salt air was eating away the sub-frame. A letter came from the owners of the site: they were legally empowered to ask tenants to update their chalets every ten years; since my father had not changed his in twenty-three, would he now proceed towards purchase of a new one or surrender his site? Starting prices for chalets were

85,000 pounds, and they could offer as a discount what he had originally paid for his, 2,200 pounds. He had until the end of the year to comply. My father agonized, took legal advice, manoeuvred and begged, but failed to earn a reprieve. He drove down finally one short December day, emptied the chalet and watched them remove its two dismantled halves.

Later he gave me some of the contents he'd rescued: a spade, a Frido, a game of petanque, a red Elastoplast tin, a pair of binoculars, our old water-skis and ski-rope. But not the yellow plastic outdoor sleeping-bags: he had put those somewhere safe for future use.

Diary

Monday 9 December

Midwinter half-light. The hardest frost of the year, and every-thing has ground to a halt, the ponds frozen, the trees under arrest, the canal locks locked. The sun can do nothing about this. It lies all day on its bed of hills, then sinks red-faced behind Pendle. It can't get up. It can't get up.

My father is no weaker today, no more comatose. He drinks a raw egg mixed with sherry. He gets to the shower unaided. He sits in his armchair in the living-room and says: 'What a marvellous family we are.' It looks to me that he will last a few more days, weeks, even months, and I must go back to London. I sit with him as long as I can, the brief light fading behind his shoulder, knowing there is a risk I may not see him again. I kiss my mother at the door and she nods: yes, if I don't make it in time she'll keep the body there.

My brother-in-law drives me to the station. We talk about whether a sudden death is better than a drawn-out one, and what 'better' means here, better for the living or the dying. We talk about my father's sense of family—his failure to let go of his children, his assumption that he had a perfect right to invade whatever space they had, even as adults: how he would walk in on Gill and Wynn without knocking, take over projects of theirs, organize them without bothering overmuch if this was what they wanted.

'I used to go at him hammer and tongs about it,' says Wynn. 'I've never taken to this family lark. You grow up and leave home and have your own children: that's family. But he thinks it means him too—everyone together—so he's a right to poke his nose in. We've had some real barneys, some right ding-dongs. But I respect him. I'll miss him.'

I remember the story of one of these fights, no more than a year ago. My father, back from the pub, had been walking around the outside of the house late at night, in his version to take the dog out, in Wynn's 'to check up on us.' Wynn, also back from the pub, had shouted at him—a long catalogue of grievances, including, most recently, the dispute they'd had over Wynn's proposal to borrow my father's Hymobile for a golfing weekend, with an unspecified number of mates. A slanging match started. My Dad took a swing, and missed. Wynn put his fists up, and they traded a few threats and expletives. My father wasn't used to fights: I couldn't remember him ever having had one, not even with me—we both seemed to have a talent for avoiding them, a fear of pain or disgrace. Yet here he was squaring up against his son-in-law, unable to make himself scarce. Luckily, Wynn's heart wasn't in it either. There may have been a couple more perfunctory or intended-to-miss swings. But soon enough they'd fallen crying in each other's arms.

I wait on Skipton station. SOVIET UNION DECLARED DEAD says the front page of the *Independent*. It is not four yet but dark already and extraordinarily cold—colder and darker than I remember the world seeming before. The trains are all fucked-up: a deep freeze in the north, an overhead line down in Northamptonshire, arson in the signal-box at London Bridge.

I'm due home in four hours. It takes me eight.

Tuesday 10 December

Piece in the newspaper about the prevention of bowel cancer. Colonic irrigation therapist Katherine Monbiot says: 'Unless you're having three bowel movements a day, you're retaining stuff in there which becomes very toxic. Some people have forty pounds of impacted faeces in their colons, getting thicker, like tyre rubber.'

I talk on the phone to Angela Carter, who has lung cancer. She's very open about it: friends want to know how she is, so she tells them, even if the news is bad. I ask her if she wants to review a new book by Raymond Carver, and she laughs, and begins to denounce Carver for the quietism and defeatedness of his characters, their dignified acceptance of the way things are. I realize later she is also talking about his quiet dignity when he died of lung cancer at fifty, and how she, the same age, intends to be different—perhaps even to rage and behave badly. I tell her about my father and add, not wanting to whine: 'Well, he's seventy-five.'

'My father died at ninety,' she says, 'and in some ways that was much worse than if he'd died at sixty.'

She agrees to take on, instead of Carver, a history of anarchism. (Later—about a month later—she rings from hospital: 'I'm going to have to cry off anarchism. They've just tipped me the black spot.')

Wednesday 11 December

The Great Freeze all over England. Temperatures ten below. Six die in motorway pile-ups. All train services between Leeds and King's Cross suspended. Impacted ground. I think of Harry Lime's funeral in *The Third Man*: 'It was February,

123

and the gravediggers had been forced to use electric drills to open the frozen ground in Vienna's Central Cemetery.' Will they have to use electric drills for burials up in Skipton? Do they have special undersoil heating, as at football grounds? It's as well my father has asked to be cremated.

Progress report last night. He drank some tea when he woke, managed an egg for breakfast, and had a gin and mixed (teaspoon-size) in the evening. But he was too weak to sit in the living-room. And when he went to the toilet, he could not get up again. My mother had to call a friend, a nurse, from down the village. The two of them lifted and dragged him back to bed.

I turn up the passage in *Sons and Lovers* where Paul and Annie Morel giggle like schoolchildren as they mix their mother a mug of milk and crushed morphine pills. They pretend it is a new sleeping draught from the doctor. 'Oh, but it is bitter,' she complains, before falling into eternal sleep.

We shiver under the raw, wide, starlit sky.

Thursday 12 December

He seems to be on a plateau of some kind, or slowly falling ground: each day a little weaker, but getting enough food down to last some more. My mother went out yesterday to buy panty-pads for him. I remember her delicately wiping his bottom the day I left, and how the soiled sheets so distressed him, though there wasn't much, just babyfudge. Ten below again: no trains to get up by, even if I was needed. The GP said yesterday he thought he might go on for six weeks yet, even three months: you just can't tell. My mother worries that he seems to be breathing through his nose as well as his mouth now; she thinks he will die at Christmas 'and spoil it for everyone,' as if it wasn't going to be spoilt anyway, or mattered this year, or as if his death would be more copable with if it happened at some other point in the calendar.

Freezing fog. A consultant in Hampshire charged with attempted murder after allegations of euthanasia. A Kennedy cleared of rape in Florida. An animal rights campaigner accused of masturbating a dolphin. Going through my desk, I find a letter my father must have sent me months ago. 'Dr P. B. Morrison' it says on the envelope: he is the only person in the world to address me as Doctor; it's been the chief benefit of my Ph.D—to allow him to believe I've followed in his path after all. Inside the envelope is a typed copy of a letter he submitted to his local Conservative MP: scrawled across the top, in handwriting, for me, it says: 'I know you don't want to hear my political views but I hope you will take the trouble to read this from beginning to end and see where we differ. Perhaps you could even submit it to your letters page, leaving out my name and address, just signed: A Northerner.' It's the letter of a disaffected Tory: why is British economic growth worse than that of countries which *lost the war*? Why is industry in decline? Hasn't there been too much public and private borrowing? Can't they think again about the poll tax? There's his usual bee-in-the-bonnet stuff about left-wing infiltrators, but also this: 'You may consider that I sound like a Socialist, which I am emphatically not, but I do go out and about quite a lot and I listen to Joe Public. Many of us feel that the government is living in a world apart and creating greater and greater differences in standards.' Maybe I've gone soft because he's so ill, but I find myself agreeing. I doubt if I'll admit it to him, though.

Last night, in the ice-darkness, terrible squawks and howls, like somebody slaughtering their pet goose for Christmas. More likely a fox taking a hen or chicken. Today a friend in Blackheath village confirms, yes, it would have been a fox, a female—mating, though, not murdering: 'Those fucking foxes and their death-throes.'

Friday 13 December

A letter from an old schoolfriend ends: 'Send my love to your parents, too. I always had a soft spot for your dad, even though he was a domineering old sod.'

I ring my mother twice. The morning report is good: he is weaker, but drank nearly a pint of milk; he intends to get up and have a shower. The evening report is less good: he moved no further than the commode by the bed; the doctor came and said the bases of his lungs were getting heavy; he is running a temperature of a hundred, and though this might be to do with his electric blanket being turned up high (as it has been for the past week: she has noticed the red burn-marks across his thigh), it could be pneumonia—the beginning of the end. She will ring in the morning and tell me if I should come. I resolve to anyway, drinking several whiskies and fretting that I won't get there in time, that he will die tonight, Friday the thirteenth.

I go to bed with Tennyson, and find this, in 'Maud':

Strange, that the mind, when fraught
With a passion so intense
One would think that it well
Might drown all life in the eye,—
That it should, by being so overwrought,
Suddenly strike on a sharper sense
For a shell, or a flower, little things
Which else would have been past by!
And now I remember, I,
When he lay dying there,
I noticed one of his many rings

126

(For he had many, poor worm) and thought
It is his mother's hair . . .
Who knows if he be dead?
Whether I need have fled?

The peeling of the senses by grief: I suppose it's true. (But no consolation.)

Saturday 14 December

The phone goes at six-forty. It is dark, and feels like the middle of the night, and I know it must be about my father and I think he is dead. He isn't, but my mother's anxious to get me there quickly: his two-day-old cough is much worse, he is drowsier and mumblier, she doesn't think it will be long. I make a cup of tea, get dressed, stagger out in the dark, the streets so icy I skitter about with my briefcase, overnight bag and the plastic carrier full of Christmas presents. The Blackheath train is fifteen minutes late, it's ten minutes at London Bridge before there are even any listings on the tube destinations board, but somehow I make it to King's Cross to catch the eight-ten, the first Leeds train of the day, the last person on, with twenty seconds to spare. I want to get straight on the phone to my father in triumph—he loves these *extraordinary piece of luck* stories.

I remember two of his. One is about flying into or home from the Azores, with a group of RAF officers: they had lined up to be parcelled out between two planes—the man in front of him was the last to get on the first plane, which went down killing all aboard. The other luck-story, scarcely a life or death matter but related in the same solemn tone of there-but-for-the-grace-of-God, concerned a camera smuggled through customs: 'I put down three bags in front of the customs officer. He said: I'll search this one and this one. Nothing. He zipped them up again, never looked at the middle bag, and off

I went.' What would my father's life have been without these little scams and victories? Not his life, anyway. What will my life be like without his stories of them? Not mine.

It is cloudless again. Mist lies in hollows. A foal stands wispily beside its mother. Across from me, a young British-Chinese businessman, twenty-five-ish, with a mobile telephone and Game Boy, argues long and bitterly with the guard about the injustice of not being able to buy a Saver Fare on the train, then spends the disputed twenty pounds twice over on a long phone call retailing the incident to his sister. The train sits endlessly outside Leeds station, but my luck's in again, I catch the Skipton connection with two minutes to spare. White paint flakes from a signal-box. The sheep-pens are full again between Shipley and Crossflatts. At Keighley station I look across to the spot where I stood two Saturdays since. It seems —is—a lifetime ago. The Monday before that was the investigatory op. The Thursday after he sat for three hours at his computer. How quickly it has come to this—me on a train back, knowing he may already be dead by the time I get there, a race against death which he can't win even if I don't lose.

The Joy of Lech

A SKIING TRIP to Lech, Austria. Long after the time most parents would have written off their children as surly adolescents scarcely to be endured even for a weekend, and long after the time most children would be holidaying only with their contemporaries, here we all are for a fortnight together, father, mother, daughter, son. Friends at university have spoken enviously of the wonderful *après-ski* life awaiting me—drink, parties, drugs, girls—but I can't see how I'm going to come by all this with my parents inhibitingly omnipresent and my sister, supposing I did get away from them, lumberingly in tow. On the slopes I'm tormented by glimpses of beautiful faces and long hair streaming from bobble caps. In the long waits for the lift or cable-car, I dream how this evening I will come upon her at the bar, the special one I have been waiting for. But the accommodation is a 'small family hotel'; my sister and I seem to be the only humans aged between nine and forty-nine; the disco action is somewhere else in town, not here. At least there's nothing to distract me from my work: while everyone else is sitting in the bland pine-and-whitewash meliorism of the hotel lounge, I keep sneaking back to my bed to read a bit more Marlowe or Tourneur or Webster, blackness and murder, infinite torture in a little room.

'*There* you are,' my father says, from the doorway of the twin-bedded room I'm sharing with him, chaps–chaps/girls–girls being the way my parents—or, rather, *he*—has chosen to divide things up, instead of husband–wife/daughter–(third room or dividing curtain) son. 'Bit antisocial wasn't it to skip off like that? We didn't know where you'd gone.'

'I said, Dad. I've got this work to do.'

'Well if you said, I never heard, you mumble so much. Look at you: unshaven, scruffy hair, in need of fresh air and exercise.'

'I wouldn't be getting that in the bar, would I?'

'Don't get smart with me. We're all family together. Come on, it's time to eat.'

At the next table sit a pair of middle-aged Scottish women, who when greeted by my father—'Nice day on the slopes? Snow to your liking?'—seem even bonier, pricklier and more dour than they were last evening.

'Rather puir conditions. And the queues to the chair-lift wair tairrible. We took a little lunch: would you believe it, two sandwiches and two lemon teas came to over five pounds?'

These ladies are on the same package as ourselves, and I wonder whether their relentless itemizing of the holiday's shortcomings have contributed to yesterday's sudden departure of the tour rep—a muddly fuzz-blonde from Manchester—to 'a meeting back at head office.' The Scottish ladies turn disapprovingly back to their meal. I reach for another glass of Liebfraumilch.

'Dr Morrison, I presume?'

A young woman is standing beside the table. She is tall, dark, with big sensual lips, heavy make-up, a long nose and hair down to her shoulders. She looks as if she has just stepped out of one of those plays I've been reading, or dreams I've been dreaming.

'I'm Rachel Stein, your new rep. This must be your family. I hope you're all having a good holiday.'

'Smashing, love,' says my father, pulling over an extra chair beside him and ordering her a drink before she has time to refuse. He takes it upon himself to fill her in on the hotel, the town, the best ski-lifts to use, the restaurants to avoid, the deficiencies of the laundry system. He also fills her in on where we live, what he does, what we're all called, our ages, our stages-in-life. When he talks proudly of me at school and now university, I wait for recognition to flare in her eyes, for her to acknowledge the feeling which I'm feeling and she surely must also feel. But she looks back to my father. A second drink arrives. The Scottish ladies, her other charges, to whom she has nodded a brief hello, look on frostily as she begins to talk. She is due to read English at Bristol University next autumn, she says, but is having a year off first—the travel company which took her on has a super scheme for reps, a month here, six weeks there, always on the move, she had Agadir in Morocco last, and it will be Greece next. She's used to moving around: her father worked abroad a lot, his firm would uproot him every two years, she spent much of her childhood on planes between boarding-school and home.

Her eyes swim suddenly: 'My father died last year. My mother thought it would do me good to get away, though I miss her.'

She is on her third beer. We are on sweet and coffee. I am in love, and she has barely looked at me yet. How artful of her to seem to be so interested in my boring old Dad, not me. Suddenly she's up and gone in pursuit of the Scottish ladies—'must catch a word with them: they're sisters you know, the Misses Laidlaw from Kirkcaldy.' We watch her swanning off into the distance.

'Always a good idea to get on with the rep,' my father says.

'Nice girl—she'll look after us.'

She certainly looks after him. Over the next evenings it becomes a ritual for her to join us at the table, and for my father to relate the events of the day, every little skiing feat and mishap. Even with half a bottle of wine inside me, I'm out of my mind with embarrassment at his banal chat (how does she hide how bored she must be feeling?), and veer between looking away in shame and trying to catch her eye. She speaks often of her poor little rich girl's childhood, and I want to take her away from all this and comfort her in her pain and loss. I wait vainly for my mother to help me out by signalling some disapproval of my father's monopolizing of her. I wait vainly for my father to say: 'Why don't you young people take off for the evening?' But he's too obsessed with Rachel, even by his own obsessive standards, to let her go. Despairingly, I join my mother and sister in the television room while my father and Rachel sit on high stools at the bar.

Back in our room, my father's snores reverberating round the pine and whitewash, I think of how the bit of him that wants the best for me, makes things easy for me, takes pride in me, is up against a different, more competitive bit I haven't admitted to seeing before. Last June, when he came to collect me at the end of my first year at Nottingham, he insisted we play squash, which I had recently—at his encouragement, seeing my face pasted by two terms of parties and drugs and seances—taken up: 'Perfect game for busy people: short, sweet and very active. I got quite good at it myself when I was a medical student.' He turned up at the hall of residence with his shorts and racquet, and, seeing friends of mine slumped about the place, with nothing better to do, he insisted they come along and watch. I anticipated a gentle, non-competitive knock-up as the best thing for both of us: I'd not slept the night before, and he hadn't (he claimed) played for twenty-five years.

But after a few minutes' limbering up, he said 'What about a game then?' He was stiff and erratic, and though I'd have liked to have been feeling more in control of my play, I knew I was losing mainly out of gallantry and that, if I let him have the first game, I should be able to crank things up in the second and third.

What I hadn't reckoned with was me getting worse and he more confident. But as he cracked his shots low and irretrievably into the court's four corners, or sent me scrambling in nausea after one of his feinted drop-shots, and the whoops and ironies echoed from the dozen or so invitees in the gallery, I realized that he was simply better than me at this, that I was not only not going to beat him, but was going to be trounced. He eased off a bit towards the end to give me a chance, but that only made me angrier and more wayward than ever. He took the third and final game with a shot against the back wall which fell, unliftingly and unliftably, on the opposite one. He shook my hand and said: 'I thought you'd have run me closer than that.'

Now, as his snores vibrate through me, I see this is what it's been like for at least five years now. I learned to water-ski; so did he. I invited friends down to our North Wales caravan; somehow, on those weekends, he always happened to be there. I talked them into going for midnight swims; he was the first out into the night-cold in trunks and towel. Lately I've mentioned a vague plan to go to Canada, to read for an MA, after I've graduated. 'Great,' he said: 'Gill and Mummy and I will sail out and join you. We'll buy a Dormobile and get it kitted out and we can tour North America. I'll have four months off and hire a locum. Why not?' Why not, except that this was a man who, when I was small, never had time for a holiday; why not, except that the whole point of Canada is to get away from him. It isn't just a matter of his not letting go, but of needing to prove himself better. When is the old bugger going to admit he's old? Why does he make me feel, and behave like, the old one? I sink a little deeper into Webster. Next thing my father will be telling me he's given up medicine and applied to read English at Nottingham.

Not quite: the next thing he does is to announce, when he wakes up, that he has strained his back in some way, that he thinks it unwise to ski today, and in any case fancies a day off sitting on his balcony in the sun. My mother jokes, as the three of us troop off to the slopes, that he'll 'no doubt be seeing his girlfriend.' It is the kind of thing she's said before, about other women he's latched on to, as if calling them 'girlfriends' is her way of convincing herself that they aren't. I leave my mother and sister on the nursery slopes and join my own class higher up. We're practising parallel turns, and with my father absent I seem to get the hang at last. After lunch, on the chair-lift, I become fascinated by the figure in the chair ahead as she reclines languidly and unfazed above all that empty air, long blonde hair pouring from beneath her hat. I prepare myself to say something as I come in behind her at the landing stage. I'll quote Eliot maybe, 'Here in the mountains you feel free,' and then, if she seems uncomprehending, the German bits—'*Frisch weht der Wind/Der Heimat zu,*' terribly genteel and polyglot. She's almost into the station now, that last bit where the chair tips to a new angle and you jump off before it hurtles forward. I swing my bar up in readiness to leap out. Twenty yards ahead of me she alights and turns and as I open my mouth to Waste-Land her I see she has bad acne and a large belly. I also see that she is a man.

Back in the room, at dusk, my father and Rachel are sitting on the balcony: they have drinks in their hands and are smoking and, with the mountains and ice-blue skies beyond, look like a Martini advertisement. I pour myself a whisky. My

mother begins to witter about our time on the slopes, and they
listen politely, like a married couple smiling condescendingly at
a nanny or grandma's account of her day out with the little
ones. I look at the bed—unrumpled, but they'd have had time
to straighten it, so who can tell. I feel a sudden disgust—not just
with him, for stealing Rachel before I could even get hold of
her, but with her, for her sophistication and cosmopolitanism
and orphan's wide-eyed fascination with an older man. As soon
as I can, I flounce off to read some more of *The White Devil*:

> To dig the strumpet's eyes out; let her lie
> Some twenty months a-dying; to cut off
> Her nose and lips, pull out her rotten teeth;
> Preserve her flesh like mummia, for trophies
> Of my just anger! Hell, to my affliction,
> Is mere snow-water . . .

Dinner is special. It's fondue evening, and Rachel has
encouraged us to choose it as an alternative to the usual drab
three courses—'all part of the package.' The Scottish ladies join
us. In the witchy candlelight, two fondue pots bubble on spirit
lamps and the seven fondue forks look like the forks devils hold
in medieval paintings. We spear chunks of French bread and dip
them into the creamy sauce, Emmenthal and Gruyère melted in
wine, herbs, garlic, lemon juice, Kirsch and cornflour. 'There's
a tradition,' says Rachel, 'that if a man drops his bread in the
sauce, he must buy a bottle of wine.' My father dips his fork in
and it comes up empty. Rachel laughs. Even the Misses Laidlaw
laugh: they've been persuaded to have some of the first two
bottles, and now we're ordering a third. As we finish the bread
and cheese, the waiters bring new pots, salad bowls and a dish
of meat chunks: we dip the meat in boiling oil, then into a
choice of sauces, Béarnaise, Andalouse, rémoulade. The heat
and candlelight, the talk and laughter, the wine and bread and

meat, melt the distances between us. We're one flesh, dipping in and out of each other's lives.

'There's another tradition,' says Rachel, 'that if a woman's fork comes up empty she must kiss all the men at the table. Come on Mrs M, be a sport.' My mother won't play along, and nor, I hope, will any of the other four women, not even Rachel, not like this, not here, round a table where 'all the men' means my father and me. The mood stiffens a little, and the fourth bottle of wine, far from easing it, seems to heighten the tension. The cherry tarts to follow lie untouched. The *bonhomie*'s gone. The waiter brings the bill.

'I'll pay for the wine,' says my father, 'and Rachel's meal is on the house, so if I divide the rest, your share'—this to the Scottish ladies—'will be a third, won't it.'

'But we thought it was *all* on the house,' says Miss Laidlaw.

'You alleged it was pairt of the package, Miss Stein,' says the other Miss Laidlaw.

'Instead of the usual evening meal.'

'At no extra charge.'

'I'll go and see,' says Rachel, disappearing into the kitchen. My father tries soothing the Misses Laidlaw: a third of the charge, with his bearing the cost of all the wine, will be in the region of twenty pounds, no more.

'Twenty pounds?'

'If she'd said ten pounds a head, we'd cairtinly have refused.'

Rachel returns. 'I'm sorry, it is a special meal, you see, and they have to charge or they can't offer it to residents. The people who come in from the town pay much more than you will—the allowance for your evening meal has been deducted.'

'But we didn't know we'd have to pay,' says Miss Laidlaw.

'And if we'd known we'd not have had it,' says the other.

There's an awkward pause.

136

'The trouble with you,' a voice is saying angrily to Rachel, 'is that you don't think. It's never crossed your mind what it's like to be someone who saves hard to come on holiday. You shouldn't have made airy-fairy promises. Not everyone is as well off as you.'

There's silence. Everyone seems a bit shocked by the voice. I'm especially shocked, because the voice appears to be mine. And it's not finished yet.

'All week we've listened to how you suffered as a child because your parents were always on the move and you had to fly back from boarding-school during holidays to visit them. Well, a lot of people would think themselves bloody lucky to go to posh schools or fly in an aeroplane at all. You've no idea, have you? We've sat here eating under false pretences. We thought you were looking after our interests, like a rep should. You've led us on.'

More silence. Rachel looks close to tears. It's the first time I've spoken more than a sentence to her and I have come on more priggishly than three generations of the Laidlaw clan could have.

In the end my father offers to pay for the whole meal, but the Misses Laidlaw, whether shocked or cheered by my blast, will have none of it, and come up with the twenty pounds. Rachel looks away, as if I'd never said a word to her, which only makes it worse. I slink off to bed. *Serves that rich bitch right* a part of me is saying, but it's a very small part compared to the huge raw-shamed part that says: *You utter prat. You'll never get to sleep with her now.*

When I wake next morning, my father's not there. I find him with my mother, in her room. They're giggling together. There's an odd pranky collusiveness between them.

'Shall we do it now?' my father asks.

'Yes, ring her,' my mother says.

'What's this about?' I ask.

'You'll see—just keep a straight face.'

My father dials three numbers. 'Could you come to Kim's room,' he mutters bleakly into the receiver. 'Something terrible has happened.'

Rachel is up two minutes later. She looks pale, worried, no make-up, her face the colour of a Russian winter, her lovely black hair without its sheen.

'What happened?' she asks.

'There was this man on the balcony,' my mother says, sitting on the bed, her head bowed, wringing her hands.

'When was this?'

'Last night, when I came back to my room—Gillian was already asleep, thank God.'

'What did he do?'

'He just stood there.'

'He didn't come in?'

'No.'

'But you were frightened? You thought he was going to come in?'

'More than that.' My mother looks down at her hands. 'He . . . you know.'

'You mean he exposed himself?'

'Yes, he got out his, you know, and just stood there.'

'What did you do? Did you ring reception? You should have rung reception, or screamed, or something.' Rachel is sitting on the bed beside my mother, stroking her hands.

'I was going to, but next thing he disappeared.'

'But this is terrible. You must have been horribly frightened. You didn't sleep?'

'No.'

'Right,' says Rachel, getting up from the bed, 'I'm going straight down to reception to report it and to get on to the police.'

'There's one other thing you should tell them,' my father says.

'What's that?'

'That it's April the first.'

'Sorry. I'm not with you.'

'It's April Fool's day.'

'I still don't . . . '

'You've been April-fooled,' my father says. 'Kim made it up, it didn't happen, it's a story, we were having you on, love.'

Rachel sits down on the bed again and bursts into tears.

They give her coffee, calm her down, say: 'There, there, you've had a nasty shock, love,' themselves shocked that the joke has worked too well. She still really doesn't see it, and nor do I see my father's motive. For my mother to invent a tale of sexual violation made sense: it's probably what she's been feeling for several days. But the idea had come from my father, not my mother—and what was in it for him? Is it because he slept with Rachel and wanted to punish himself for it—the joke as atonement? Or that he hasn't slept with her and wants to punish her for it—the joke as revenge?

We leave for the airport that evening. In reception, as we stand among our cases, Rachel kisses us all, but there's a wariness and distance about her: she seems young and vulnerable, not the worldly sophisticate to whom we have, in our different ways, been horrible.

'TTFN,' my father says.

'Take care, all of you,' she shouts back.

Some months later, my parents show me a letter they've had from Rachel, describing her first term at Bristol University. It is, I'm relieved to find, shallow, childish and untouched by feeling.

Death

MY MOTHER STANDS at the door. I know from her face that he is still alive—and from his, as I rush past her, that he won't be for long. He is asleep, though awake or asleep is hard to tell. Asleep, his right eye won't quite close, and I can see the rolled-up white of the ball. Awake, he can't open his left eye fully—the lid stays low and hooded over the pupil. His cheeks are hollower. His chin, with its week-old stubble, is an offence to his philosophy of close shaving. He is breathing simultaneously through his mouth, which falls in a kind of rigid open slackness, and his nose—I can see the contractions just under the bridge, the skin tightening as he snuffs fiercely for air. His bottom lip falls away from his teeth. Something pink is gumming them up—bits of unswallowed or regurgitated pills. His hair drops long and sleekly over the tops of his ears—it just doesn't seem to have got the idea; it keeps on growing regardless.

He is propped high on the bed, to keep his lungs clear. I feel I am looking not at him but at his death-mask—something to do with the puffiness of the eyes. He has always had huge pouches under his eyes, leather purse-size, and now they are pouchier still. I sit in the chair next to him, catching a reek from the bedclothes. I hold his hand, the one unshrunken part of

140

him, still so big and autocratic and can-do. I can see the holes
and crevices opening up in him—above his collar-bone,
between his ribs, under his ears—as the skeleton seems to move
up through him to the surface of his skin, in charge, taking
possession, turning out the flesh. I lift the sheet and see the pads
under him and the nappy round his middle, its two sticky-tape
ties at the side. He is far gone from himself, yet the breathing is
deep and regular. I thought that he could not shrivel further,
could not become any more ill, but I was wrong.

All his adult life he has spent among medicines and now he
is going to die among them. They sit like nurses on the
window-sill—Diconal, Frusemide, Largactil, Periactin—not the
old glass jars and coloured bottles and round cardboard pill-
boxes of his first postwar practice, but white plastic containers
with push-and-screw safety lids. There seems nothing odd
about them being there, only that they're for him. His home
has always been an overspill for pills and equipment from
surgery—he liked to be on the safe side, to have spares and
duplicates to hand, not least for his own family. For a time,
when I was twelve, he had given me small plastic syringes to
play with, a sixties advance on the old metal ones—with the
needles snapped off, they made good water-pistols, and I'd
found them a nice little earner, selling them to schoolfriends for
a shilling or florin according to size. When word got back he
was furious and stopped the supply: it wasn't my capitalistic
enterprise he minded but the fact that I was a doctor's son—
what if people gossiped that Arthur Morrison was using his son
in this way to make a bob or two?

The newest syringes, which he has by his bed now, are
smaller and more disposable still: they come with a glass
capsule, and you break the end off, dip in and fill your needle,
administer the injection and throw them away. The medicines
he can't take by mouth he takes in this way from my mother: a

quick swab of the thigh, the prick of the needle barely registering in his eyes (because he is too drugged? because there is too much pain elsewhere to notice a pinprick?). The left thigh is now blotchy with needle-marks: he is bleeding gently from one of them and my mother washes the blood away.

I leave him asleep and walk through to the living-room where David and Vera Whitehouse are drinking coffee, having driven down from Redcar for a last visit—it is thirty-three years since they left Earby, after David's twelve months as a trainee, but they've kept up the relationship. We shake hands, and agree how sad it is, how sudden, how Arthur has always been so fit and active, all that. And then they're brisk in a way my mother and I need: it seems to them, both of whom have done work with terminal cancer patients, that he has no more than forty-eight hours to live—do we have any morphine? There are patients who get very restless, panicky, even violent at some point in their last hours, who are climbing up the wall in pain one minute and dead a few hours later. With his lungs clogging up, my father might react this way too, and we will have to have something to sedate him. Do we have all we need —syringes, morphine, Largactil? And then, having sorted us out, the Whitehouses are off: it is a two-hour drive back, and they've stayed only half an hour, but this is what impending death demands, what people give in friendship and tribute, what my father would give, had given, too.

Half an hour later, he gets himself upright on the edge of the bed. This is his single obsession now, to keep his chest vertical—everything else, even the drugs schedule, has been forgotten. Every hour he wakes and struggles up; even asleep he leaves his right leg dangling over the edge in readiness, and we put a chair with its back against the bedside to prevent him falling out. Upright now, he's mumbly, breathless and wants a drink. Under the sheet I can see his lumpy belly with its rip of stitches—like the wolf in the children's story who swallows the goat-kids, falls asleep, and wakes to find its stomach full of stones. I hold a half-pint tankard of iced water for him—not one of his old silver golf club tankards (burglars had made off with those), but a glass one with a red fox-hunting motif in a panel on its side, one of a set I drank my first bitter shandy from, at his behest ('Learn the taste of beer now, and you won't go wild later'), when I was twelve. I put a towel under his chin, and tip his head back, and he forces a bit down, and a lot more comes back up, his hands shaking as he tries to steady them round the glass. 'Is that better?' I ask, and he manages 'Yes,' and then I try him with a straw, aiming its end between his teeth, and he gets the idea, seems too weak at first to draw anything up, but then makes a stupendous effort, the indents under each ear drawn in fiercely as he sucks, sucks. A drop of water makes it into him, and as he struggles for breath again I imagine, no, *hear*, this drop of water he's swallowed pinballing down and through and into the dry places inside.

His burnt lips look moister now, his voice-box is oiled and working again, though I can't make out what he's saying. My mother, responding, chats and flirts and teases, and there are certain words she says at which he seems to prick up. He had said to her in the night, 'Could you move me, pet,' and that *pet* has convinced her he knows she is there and recognizes her still, but I can't say with confidence, or even without it, that he recognizes me. His eyes have milked up, distant, unfocusing. I had hoped he would know me one more time, but it doesn't look likely now. If the point of my coming here was for that recognition, to get some sort of return for my nursing and attending, there is no longer a point, for he's off on his own. There is a Robert Frost poem which says this, or some of it, or more than it:

> . . . *The nearest friends can go*
> *With anyone to death, comes so far short*
> *They might as well not try to go at all.*
> *No, from the time when one is sick to death,*
> *One is alone, and he dies more alone.*

As we help him back on to the bed now, lifting him under the arms, his body so wasted away yet so heavy with fluid, and as we heave his bottom (BTM he used to call it, a euphemism for a euphemism) closer to the pillows to keep him upright, and as we swing his legs back up and straighten him, I wonder whether these manoeuvres are more a comfort to us—an illusion of *doing something*—than they can ever be to him. Perhaps if he had bedsores, our tending, even at this late stage, could provide some relief to him. But now he has got near to a place so far away that what's happening to him here no longer seems to register.

There are to be no more moments of lucidity, no more conversations, only the look of him all afternoon and evening: the stubble, the left eye half-open, the head sunk on his chest until some word in whatever anecdote we are trying to engage him with—my train journey up, my mother's dealings with the gardener—seems to catch and snag for a second, to trip some not always related words of his own, then to ratchet away hopelessly into space again. Yesterday he had drunk some milk and asked: 'Can I have some more wine?' Even that sort of irreality, that hallucidity, seems unattainable now.

As the day drags on, it becomes harder to ignore the stench coming from his bed. Finally, around teatime, with my sister there and a few drinks inside us, we resolve to change him. It means my catching him under the armpits, lifting him up and off the bed, then turning him through 180 degrees to plonk him on his bedside chair. While I hold him there, my mother clears the pads, the soiled cotton sheets, the swimming rubber sheet underneath, and my sister puts down new sheets in their place. Then we unsnap the ties on his nappy, and I lift him upright again while my sister slides it off: it peels away crooked and slantwise, snagging on his thigh, but at least the wiping of his bottom, which is smudgy but not sore, need be no more than perfunctory. Then we slide the new nappy under him, my sister proficient at one side, my mother—a fifties terry-nappy mother—struggling with the technology at the other. I have to slide my right arm through my father's right arm and across his chest to support him under the left arm, while with my free left arm I hold the nappy firm so my mother can stick down the tie. Now he is done, and I begin to lift and turn him in a semicircle back again. But to do this means moving the chair with my knee, and I miscue and tilt it, and for one horrible moment one of its legs catches his leg, spearing the instep, pressing hard into the puffiness, skewering him to the floor, enough for him to mumble: 'Chair'. Then I see and lift it off again, and I get him up and then recumbent on the bed, his chest vertical, the pillows propped behind him. And I sit there breathing heavily, his hand in my hand, wondering if he, being the patriarch he was, ever changed a nappy of mine, and wondering if this might be a definition of what it is to be grown up—not changing your child's nappy but changing your parent's.

When I walk my sister back in the dark, clear skies again, I say: 'I hope he dies tonight. I don't want him to go on any more.'

'I hope so too.'

'Shall we ring if he does?'

'No—in the morning.'

'The only two mongol children I delivered,' my mother says, over her whisky, 'were both to girls in their twenties. One was a mild case, a happy boy, really, the other died of pneumonia at six months. It just goes to show, it's not only women over forty. These days they can catch them, and give terminations. I referred girls for terminations, too, if that was what they wanted—rather than what their boyfriends or parents wanted. But I sometimes think, especially if the girl didn't marry and have kids later: was that right? Should I have done more to persuade her to go ahead? Of course, I always feel lucky I didn't have more Thalidomide cases—I never prescribed it myself, there was another drug I'd always used that was equally good for sickness, and I saw no reason to change it. The one Thalidomide baby I delivered was another GP's. All I can remember was having no warning there was going to be anything unusual, and the head coming out, and thinking: Jesus, what's this? The only way to describe it is that it looked like a penguin—flippers for arms, no legs, and something monstrous about its face: I saw it for only a second, but it looked like a single eye in its forehead. Another doctor, with a needle, came and took it from me—it died almost at once. It was only years later the Thalidomide scandal came out and we realized that's what we'd been dealing with. I don't think the mother ever had any idea how bad it was. She was a Mrs Molloy, and she went on to have about six kids, including one who drowned in a culvert. But the worst death like that was Jean Harrison's—remember? She left her one-year-old in the bath with her six-year-old, then the phone rang, and when she came back the baby was under the water, and the brother hadn't noticed: it was evening surgery, and Dad and I drove there at once, and he was pumping away for half an hour on the bathroom floor trying to revive her, and then the ambulance came with oxygen, but it was hopeless, hopeless.'

★

Now my mother is asleep and I sit in front of the television and watch the news (another policeman stabbed, name of Morrison), and then a film, *Escape from Alcatraz*. I fall asleep in front of it, waking in some dark and nameless hour to the sound of the phone, which I rush to knowing it must be terrible news, that my father has died at home, and then I find myself in his bedroom, where the phone by the bed is disconnected, and there he is breathing next to my mother, neither of them hearing, and I rush back into the living-room and pick up another phone—it's the GP, checking on progress and inviting us to feel free to call him any time of night at the following numbers. I thank him and hang up, wondering why he has felt free to call us at any time of night without being invited to, but then I find it is only eleven-fifteen. I wander back to my parents' bedroom. Her hand is in his, I see, like the couple in Larkin's 'An Arundel Tomb', though the little dog is not at their feet but in the kitchen, and both are flesh and blood, not a monument, though one may be tomorrow. My eyes fill at the sweetness of her hand in his, sleeping beside each other as they have for forty-five years, love surviving them.

But then my father seems half to wake, and tries to move his hand from hers, needing to get upright, can't understand what is loading his arm down. My mother wakes too, and we get him up, and he asks for ice. Ice in a glass? No, he shakes his head, just ice, and my mother comes back with two slivers of it which we stuff into his mouth. He keeps them there, superhuman, clenched between his teeth, and his voice is lubricated again and he asks, 'Are you keeping the schedule?', and we laugh and say, 'Yes, Dad, all your medicines are noted down.' 'Good.' It seems the right time to sedate him, but my mother resists the morphine, makes do with the Largactil, which should knock him out for a bit all the same. I go to

147

bed, can't sleep. Within an hour I can hear his voice and when I go down he's sitting on the edge of the bed again, wanting water. Another hour, his voice again, but I leave them to it this time, and in my half-asleep state think of him there below, fighting off sedatives, an eternal life force, a fridge that will never be turned off.

I wake at six-thirty, utter blackness, and, descending the stairs —some anxiety but quietly certain he is still alive—hear the regular sniffy intakes of breath. My mother lies on her back, a copy of a large-print Dick Francis novel flat across her breast. My father is on his side, and every so often seems to want to raise himself, his right hand feeling for the edge of the bed, scrabbling to get a grip, the arm tensed. But then the hand weakens, the arm slackens, he lapses back into sleep. I go to make tea, and return to sit by the bed. My mother wakes, confused for a moment to see me there. I hand her a mug of tea, and she sits up:

'How's he been?' I ask.

'He woke at four, and sat on the edge of the bed, and coughed and coughed until he seemed to get something up and felt better. Then I gave him an injection.'

'Morphine?'

'Yes. For once he didn't ask what it was for. All he said was: "Can I lie down now?"'

I point to his frail flapping efforts to get upright: it seems cruel not to help him, but it would be crueller to sit him up when he's so weak and out-of-it. Then I notice him opening his eyes, which seem to fix on something beyond the bed, and I walk round, into his line of vision, hoping I will register in them. But nothing registers at all: his eyes are looking cloudily into some middle distance—they seem to have died. His breathing, too, has changed in some way—my mother remarks on it—slower, though still regular. Then he gives a slightly bigger breath than usual—and stops. I nod at my mother. After about half a minute, he breathes again, lightly, a wisp only, and she puts her left hand to her chest, as if to say, *Christ, what a relief, I thought he was gone.* Then nothing again. Another half minute, another wisp. Then silence. And more silence, restful. I look at his clock: seven o'clock. Then at hers: seven-ten. It is very quiet: I can hear only the distant cawing of rooks.

He is dead, and I feel an odd triumph about it. He is dead, the thing (when I was small) I used to dread more than any other, but I'm still here, my mother's still here, I can hear her breathing, the world has ended but we've survived, we're OK. He is dead—no rage against the dying of the light, no terror and delirium, only a night-light smothered in its own wax. Sitting here, the body silent between us as we peer into it for a sign of some kind, I'm on a shock-induced high. If I listen hard enough, I know I'll hear his own count-your-blessings verdict: 'Well, that wasn't so bad, was it? When I think how it could have been—drawn-out, or abrupt and messy, or in hospital rather than here—it makes me feel lucky. A good death and a good life too: who could beat it?'

'The GP said to lay him flat.' My mother rises, icy calm, and we lift his head and remove some of the pillows from under it, straighten him on his back, pull his right leg up from its dangling position, and draw the covers up to his chest— why would anyone, except in the movies, draw them over the head, and shut out before time what will soon be unseeable forever? I'm crying quietly through this, and then leave my mother alone with him, and cry more noisily at the kitchen window. Outside is a tree-stump he left as a bird-table, with frills of white fungus growing out of its side.

I keep shooting back to see how she is, to see how he is. I

feel a lifetime has passed, but the clock says seven-thirty, and here I am in the living-room, twenty, thirty minutes after his death, wading in boxes and boxes of photographs. It's something I do every Christmas, but Christmas has come a little early this year. Even now I can see it's some futile struggle to resuscitate and preserve him. His face swims up from the bendy sheens of black and white, the cardboard transparencies, the tiny sepia squares—in RAF uniform in the Azores; in his wedding suit in 1946; with a litter of twelve labrador pups, with babies, with toddlers, with his leg in plaster; being carried downstairs 'fresh' by a collection of male friends at his retirement party. There is something boyish and little in these that won't do, won't measure up. Then I find something better: a photograph of him outside our old rectory, leaning dandyishly against the side of his black Mercedes, a cigarette dangling from his right hand, his beautiful wife, fortyish then, posed beside him—an image of wealth and health and substance to set against the poverty and sickness we've lived with for the past month; an image, too, of the aspirations and affectations death has snuffed out.

My mother comes in to say that she has rung the vicar—it is not yet eight, so he can say a prayer at matins and word will get round the village without our having to phone: the church still has its uses after all. I ring my wife and children in London to give them the news, and during this my mother comes in to ask: was that me who's just been in her bedroom? Somebody had seemed to be walking about. I go through, and stand at the door, but it feels unspooky, and goes on feeling unspooky. My father, I'm sure, is too much of a materialist to become a ghost, and the room in which we've watched him die is unwaveringly bright and rational. It isn't he but we who move about like ghosts, pale and hovery and traumatized. There he lies, solid on his bed. I touch his skin. An hour after his death his forehead has cooled to marble already, but when I slip my hand under the covers and across his huge ribs, the chest is hot.

And it is still warm when the GP comes at nine: 'Poor Arthur, you didn't deserve this,' he says. And it is not much cooler—I know, I check—when Malcolm, the undertaker, arrives at eleven. He is fortyish, remembers me from school, is gangly in a grey suit with a Rotary Club badge on his left lapel: 'Oh dear, oh dear, Arthur,' he says and doesn't know where to put himself.

He asks for a bowl of water, and while my mother is out of the room uses a long tweezery implement to shove a piece of cotton wool into my father's open mouth, where it rests (visibly) at the back of the tongue—'to stop any gases coming up,' he explains. My mother returns with the warm water. Malcolm takes a razor and for the next hour or so works away at my father's week-old stubble, 'just tidying him up.' I look at my mother and see that she is thinking what I am thinking— why bother with these cosmetics? Who will see him in the coffin? And even if he were to lie open for public viewing in a chapel of rest, who would mind the stubble? He might, I suppose: he was always a great one for checking whether I'd shaved. But he didn't like this sort of shaving himself—used only an electric razor—and would have resented the waste of manpower: better to have got Malcolm out doing something useful in the garden. If he'd been here, *really* been here, that's what he'd be arranging.

But my mother and I are new to all this, and yield to Malcolm's sense of etiquette. And at least it gives him something to do while he chats:

'I've done forty-eight this year—about one a week it works out. It's a sideline, the undertaking. My main business is joinery. But I don't get much call for that these days, and you've got to make ends meet. There's nothing special you want, is there? No? Fine. Of course some people want the works, you know, the whole waxworks. It's amazing what you can do these days—inject the client with formalin by sticking this tube into the neck artery, or drain the blood and urine off with an electric pump, and put caps under the eyelids to make the eyes more rounded, sleep and peace, like. I don't hold with that: making a corpse like a plum instead of a prune, it's not right. No embellishing, nothing fancy, simple and clean: that's my philosophy.'

I wait for the moment when he will nick my father's chin—do the unpumped dead bleed less profusely than the living?—but he does it all spotlessly. I help him roll my father on to his side, so he can remove the pads from under him, wash his bottom and put a fresh nappy between his legs: it's dirty work, but someone has to do it, and 'there may be more fluids,' he says. My father's body is a little stiffer now, but his back, as I hold him, is still warm, the skin red and corrugated where the sheet has wrinkled under him. 'This is why we come in fairly sharpish,' says Malcolm, 'before the rigor mortis. After twelve hours they can be very stiff and hard to move. After four or five days they go floppy again.'

My father said that he'd never wear a shroud in his coffin; and he would not have wanted to waste a good suit. So now I help dress him in a pair of fawn cotton pyjamas. Malcolm hasn't batted an eyelid yet, any more than my father has, but suddenly he seems flustered. I hold the body upright for him. He puts the right arm in the left sleeve, only realizing his mistake when he finds the pyjama buttons are underneath my father's back. We lift the body, and get the pyjamas off then on again the right way. They won't button up over the swollen stomach and zip scar, so we leave them open. There's one final cosmetic act: the chin support, a small white plastic T to keep the jaw from dropping too far open. Malcolm has some trouble adjusting the length of this: it's either too short, leaving my father dopily open-mouthed, or too long, clamming him up, unnaturally tight-lipped. Finally he jams the stick end into the collar-bone, an awkward riving process, and I have to remind myself that this won't be hurting. My father, at any rate, looks better for it—peaceful, no teeth showing.

'I should have said earlier,' Malcolm remarks as we draw the sheets back up to the chin, hiding the T support. 'That's a pacemaker there, isn't it. I'll have to get the doctor to remove it, or come back with a scalpel myself. We have to take it out, you see, if he's being cremated: it says so on the form, no HPMs. There've been cases where they exploded.'

'I'd like to have it—if it's not going to be used by anyone else.'

'I'll check with the doctor. I'm sure it'll be fine.'

Once Malcolm has gone I sit with my father again and touch the little pacemaker box in his chest, sliding it about under the skin. Still warm, that chest, though it is six hours now since he died and for two hours he has been exposed to cold air. But the forehead is damp and Siberian. My mother sits across from me, holding his hand. She has not cried properly yet: with each phone call—and as the day wears on there are more and more of these—her eyes water and her lips tremble, but she does not howl. Now, finally, she throws herself across him and sobs into his cold neck and chest.

It is a horrendous, unfamiliar, back-of-the-throat wail. She doesn't want me there listening, and I suppress the instinct to go and hold her, knowing that if I do she will stop, and feeling sure that she should voice her pain, release it, weep it out:

> Give sorrow words: the grief that does not speak
> Whispers the o'er fraught heart, and bids it break.

So I withdraw and move restlessly about the house,

looking in on my father each time I pass his door: I've been doing this for the past fortnight and see no reason to stop now, just because he's dead. After lunch—lunch!—I come back in secret and slip my hand under the sheet: nine hours after his death, the body is dimly warm still, but there's a shock when I touch his icy hands, which unlike his face have turned white. And he is stiffer, too, not just the limbs but the skin. I stroke and clasp his fingers. When my mother comes in, she isn't shocked; she sits beside me and starts to touch him around the mouth, kneading it into positions which she likes the look of and he holds for her, as if death were a camera pose, or else a new suit he were trying on ('How do I look?), which in a sense it is.

Later she lies down next to him and falls asleep for an hour. But she spends the night in the spare bedroom, not sure whether it would be unseemly or traumatic to sleep with him. I go upstairs to my room and write a letter. I'm woken next morning at eight by a phone call from one of his patients, a woman who lost her parents in her twenties and has always been devoted to mine.

'Please tell me it isn't true. He was like a father to me. What shall I do? I've left my house to him.'

Three Visits

THE FIRST DAY of life after his death. I walk to the café on Skipton High Street where we used to come after hours, boys from the grammar school, girls from the high school, cigarettes, a jukebox, coffee. This morning, school holidays and recession, I have the place nearly to myself. My appointment at the registry office isn't till twelve.

A girl comes in, blonde, eighteenish, white see-through blouse and flowery leggings under a long coat, pushing a Maclaren buggy with a child of two inside, immaculately turned out. Shorter, younger, trim-jacketed, a boyfriend skulks behind. The girl is in charge: she slides a tray along the counter, loads it with cakes and drinks, pays at the till and turns, carrying the tray in one hand while pushing the buggy with the other. She chooses a table, parks the pushchair next to it and sits down on the green plastic bench, sliding her legs under the imitation marble tabletop. Some seconds after, as if reluctantly acknowledging he is of the same party, the boy takes the seat opposite, smug-looking, not saying a word to her, not looking at the baby either, who is churring happily with a bottle of thinned Ribena.

Is she a nanny or childminder? No, the baby calls her

'Mummy'. Is he the father? Hard to say. He doesn't seem to be a husband—neither of them wears a ring—but is he a partner? His lack of attention to both the girl and the baby is no kind of clue—it could just be shyness, or the domestic boredom of coupledom, or a northern male's assumption that pouring tea and petting babies falls outside his domain. But I can't get over how pleased with himself he looks. What's his power over the girl, that she sits there doing everything—leaning over now to wipe the face of her baby daughter, who's beginning to be restless in her pushchair straps, who's saying 'Mummy' pleadingly and wants to be out? The more the child whinges, the less a father he looks, the more that sullen-smug face of his suggests a different story: Look at me, I'm just seventeen and have an older woman who gives me her body, no trouble or lip or bills to pay. But if so, what's in it for her, what does she get from him? Her control, her copingness, seem to say: I can do better than this. But she's second fiddle to some smug, sullen, misogynistic berk.

The café has filled up a bit. I turn back to my paper, sneaking looks as the mother plays a slap-game with her daughter, a rhyming pat-a-cake routine which ends with her smacking the child's hands more vigorously than the game requires, harder than seems right. She turns to her consort, a bulge and swing in her blouse as she does so—unlike me, he looks away. Her face in profile is not a happy face, the top lip protrudes, the chin is rattily set back, more smoky anger in her than first seemed. Now the child, twenty minutes in captivity, is straining at its harness, whining, 'Lap, lap,' and the girl, tensing, worried they're becoming a spectacle, says loudly, loud enough to make people look across: 'Shut up. Wait till we're on the bus.' There's quiet for a bit, but then the child whines again, 'Mummy, lap,' not seeing what there is to wait for or why, and the whine turns into a cry, and now the girl leans over and slaps the child hard across the thighs. The child screams, less in pain than outrage, long shock-breaths between each cry. The mother and her lover sit silent and impassive, while the crying goes on under its own steam, nothing to do with them. An undeserved slap, a mother at the end of her nerves: no more than this, but there's a knot of awkwardness now, everyone in the café pretending not to have noticed but conversation faltering and silence gathering as reproach. I think of my father, soppy-stern most of the time (once, after I'd been cruel to my sister, he drew his fist back to hit me in the face but wasn't able to go through with it), occasionally a mad disciplinarian (his insistence I empty my plate, the smack I got for peeing in some bushes, the day he locked me in the cellar). What was kind and right, where did cruelty and neglect begin, what could you do that didn't damage your own life or your child's or both?

At last the girl stands up and begins to tidy cups, cutlery and napkins on to her tray. The boy, smug and wordless still, goes ahead of her to the door. The girl puts the tray down and unbrakes the pushchair—the child ceasing to cry now, aware something is happening—and out they go into the street, among other pushchairs, other people, the mill of bodies, the unending cycle of sex and parenthood, never enough time, never enough patience.

Anita M. Barnard wears a polite smile and an elegant grey dress. She likes to give a personal service, handwritten, no computerization. Friendly but not nosy, she holds a fountain pen and asks me to sit down. She needs to know, for the purposes of the form, who, when, where and how: she needs to know whether I was present at the time. But she does not want to talk about the death more than is strictly necessary, and if she ever knew my father (probably didn't—works six miles away, is under forty), she isn't letting on.

I give her his full name. The doctor's certificate says: Cause of death—Carcinoma 1(a).

'What does 1(a) mean?' I ask.

'Oh, that's a doctor's thing,' she explains. 'It means leading directly to death rather than a contributory factor, which is 1(b). When did he die?'

'Yesterday.'

She scritches away. 'Relation to the deceased?'

'Son.' I look at the map of Craven District on the wall, her patch of births, marriages and deaths. 'Are people fairly well in control of themselves by the time they come here?' I ask.

'Yes, usually, though you get some who want to talk about it and cry. Sometimes I want to cry myself in the really tragic cases—you know, like children.'

'But you don't just do deaths?'

'No, but this time of year, mostly. Today I've had four deaths, a birth and a marriage. Getting wed on a Monday morning—seems a bit odd to me, when they didn't have to, either. I'll just copy this out neatly and then we're done.'

I take the green cremation slip, the form for the DSS, the information booklets for widows, the death certificate itself. Outside on the notice-boards are the banns of intending couples. Four older men, MARR DISS, marrying younger women, SINGLE. A couple whose address is a barge on the Leeds–Liverpool canal. A twenty-two-year-old man marrying a thirty-eight-year-old woman. Not one old-fashioned marriage—people in their mid-twenties doing it for the first time. But then it's not the marrying season, not Whit or the hot blood of July. And my parent's wedding hadn't been so Mills and Boon either, by the look of the photos: registry office, half a dozen friends and relations huddled autumnally by a red brick wall, the war barely a year behind.

I shop for the wake at Morrisons, the big new supermarket where the old cattle mart used to be. My father had talked warmly of the place ('You can get any bloody thing you want') and bought shares in it, as if it were the family firm. I load the trolley high with drink—gin, whisky, brandy, vodka, rum, wine, lager, bitter, as much as I can get in, the booze mound, commemoration and amnesia. I have to hold the wine boxes at the top to prevent them falling out. A man in the queue behind me winks. The woman on the till gives a knowing smile: 'Now here's someone who's going to have a good Christmas.'

I drive to Airedale Hospital. Just along the corridor from Ward 19 is the postgraduate medical school, and in the library, among the *BMJ*s and ghoulish textbooks, I see a woman, greying, fortyish, curatorial, who may be able to help. I explain: 'My father was a GP locally for thirty-five years. When he retired he donated some equipment here. He said that they were setting up a museum. I wondered if I could look. I wanted to see his donations.'

The woman seems a bit put out: this isn't routine. 'Sorry, it doesn't mean anything to me, I'm afraid. There's no actual museum, you see. We wanted one but we haven't the resources.'

'Not even an archive or display case or something?'

'We thought it would be good to have exhibits in the main reception, but it's against fire regulations: the law says you need acres of free floorspace. What's your father's name?'

'Dr Morrison. From Earby. He retired in 1976.'

'Well I've been here twenty years and I don't remember any bequest. But we do have a storeroom where various bits and pieces are kept.'

The storeroom is taken up with old medical journals, surplus from the library. On a high shelf are some little wooden boxes, beautifully made, chestnut-gleaming, with stethoscopes and other equipment under their sliding lids. It's cold in here but the woman is slowly warming to her task.

'We did have a few doctor's bags, with bottles in—the coloured sort, with stoppers. But thieves broke in—looking for drugs, the police thought—and they whipped them: they're the sort of thing you can sell at car boot sales. There's only this one left now.'

It's leather, and old, and grey—but it's not my father's.

'That's about it, I'm afraid, except for George.' She opens the lid of a large rough wooden box and pulls out a thigh-bone. She seems to relax, as if she's forgotten my being here is an irregularity and imposition, as if she's finally interested.

'We laid him out on the steps, a doctor and me, to see if he was all there. Of course they're made of plastic these days, the modern sort, not the real thing like George here.'

She takes out another off-white branch—a rib or arm.

'People feel funny about skeletons,' she says, 'but it never bothers me, coming in here, or working next door after dark knowing he's in his box. I rather like him.'

She stows the bones back in the box, shuts the lid and locks the door behind us. I thank her for her time. I'd hoped his old medical equipment might restore some part of my father to me, but thieves in the night had got there first.

In the car I wonder: had she been right about George being George? How different are male and female skeletons? Couldn't George have been Janet?

Janet had lived in a box in our attic, in a windowless room with bookshelves on which were ancient medical textbooks

160

with colour plates of appalling skin diseases and disfigurements (at thirteen I swooned darkly over the venereal disease section and convinced myself that the slight soreness of my penis must be a syphilitic chancre). I opened the lid one day and there she was—a grinning skull and a jumble of bones. My father said he'd bought her when he was a medical student—'already dead, by the way.' He didn't know much of her history, only that she was young—and that she was a she. He showed me how you joined her up. At the top of every bone was a metal hook which clipped into the clasp at the bottom of the next bone, which in turn hooked into, and so upward and on. We didn't attempt the full assembly, and I always doubted if she was all there, whether a few bones hadn't gone walkies. But we had fun raising a leg together—femur, tibia, patella, talus. I was fixated by the skull, which had been sawn through cross-ways so that you could lift the top off, like a teapot lid. There were two little clasps on either side of the skull, exactly like the clasps on my father's King Edward cigar boxes, and little stitches or indentations ran round, like Dinky tyre tracks. The eyes were two perfect Os, but the nose was crinkly and jagged. Best of all was the jawbone, or mandible, wired up so that you could move it up and down and set her full set of teeth chomping (or did I imagine the teeth? was she just open-mouthed?)

There was nothing in the least spooky about Janet, though my father said I must be careful: 'Mind not to break any bones, and don't tell your friends about her—they might be scared.' Years later, when we started a youth club in one of the out-buildings, I removed the skull from the box and used it as a light-shade for the disco: the sixty-watt green-coloured bulb fitted through the neck and shone out through her eyes as the floor shook to Tamla Motown. I don't think anyone ever realized she was the real thing. Sometimes the skull cap seemed to overheat and smoke and smell a bit, and I'd lift the lid off and find a soot deposit in the frontal bone.

In the end, I hope, Janet found a good home, and the skull and bones got together again. Perhaps another medical student is learning from her, or she really is George in the corner at Airedale. I remember her fired up and throbbing to the latest Tamla, or imagine her on display in a lecture room, not one of those who lie dully beneath the earth but eternally spirited, a doer and teacher, the last of her kind.

Back home, the vicar calls, an anorak over his dog-collar.

'I never met Arthur, and I'm sorry about that. I've heard a lot about him. I'm sure we'd have got on.'

'He wasn't much of a churchman,' says my mother.

'No, but I know from all his activities for the village he was a Christian, if not a believer. Sometimes believers don't behave like believers, and non-believers do. The social ministry, we used to call it in college—that was Arthur.'

Old Canon Mackay, whose church I'd gone to as a boy, wouldn't have been quite so eagerly exculpating: he might have made us squirm a little over the question of a funeral service for such a resolute atheist; he would have wanted at least a show of solemnity or belief. But the new generation of vicars aren't like this: they're *nice*—charm school graduates who want to put you at your ease, to say: 'I know you don't believe in any of this God nonsense, but never mind, it shouldn't stop you going to church—after all it hasn't stopped me running one.' Or in this case: 'I know your spouse never went to church in his life, but that doesn't matter, indeed in some ways it's better: it makes the funeral all the more of a challenge.'

I remembered Terry Kilmartin's funeral from the summer and the silver-haired game show host who had presided over it. 'I never knew Terry,' he had begun ('Well, it's Mr Kilmartin to you in that case,' I could imagine the old curmudgeon barking back). Terry at least had a feeling for religion; my father's only feeling about religion was that he couldn't abide it. He didn't come to the carol services that my sister and I took part in. He didn't like singing, didn't like *sitting*. When I was nine, and wanted to join the village choir because my two best friends had done so, he did his best to talk me out of it: 'You realize it will cut into our Sundays.' I put his atheism down to his practicality and his medical training: could anyone who had ever conducted an autopsy believe in a soul? Once, though, when I was twenty or so, he had sent me a letter explaining his philosophy of life—something about a long car journey and time. There'd been an obscurantism about it which could have come from whisky and working too late at the billiard table, but which was odd for him and even a little mystical. In my callow, prissy academicism, I found the letter embarrassing and threw it in the bin. Now I wish I had it. Now it might provide some guidance. In life, he wouldn't be seen dead in church; now that he was dead, would he want us to pew it out through a parade of speciousness?

'What sort of funeral did Arthur want?' the vicar asks, on cue, from his teacup.

'Hard to say,' my mother replies. 'Keep it short, that was the main thing. No pious reminiscences. A couple of hymns only, and he didn't have any preferences because, to be honest, he couldn't have named a hymn if you'd asked. An even shorter cremation: he said we'd to scatter him round the garden. And then back to the pub for a big booze-up, and no tears.'

'That sounds all right.'

I can feel my mother struggling to honour my father's atheistic impulses, while also honouring her own religious ones: if she's to be reunited with him in the next world, he must have a proper send-off in this. 'How long do you think the service should be?' she asks. 'What's normal?'

'Twenty-five minutes is usually enough. I've known it done in fifteen.'

We run through some details and possible hymns, and then he tells me he once read a piece I wrote about Burnley football club: 'You must be the same vintage as me: McIlroy, Pointer, Adamson, Connelly. I used to go every week. I still do—with my son now.' He makes some jokes about what it's like to be a vicar at a football match—being mistaken in dog-collar for a Newcastle United supporter, saying prayers for Burnley to win, a miracle if they get promoted, etc. He sounds as if he's more at home on Saturdays than on Sundays. He puts his anorak back on and his claret-and-blue scarf. 'Ring me about the hymns. My sympathies again. I'll see you Friday.'

'What are we going to do about the kids?' my mother asks as she closes the door on him. 'I don't know if Gill will want hers there. What about you?'

'They're coming up. Kathy agrees. I've already arranged it.'

'Not much of a place for kids, a funeral.'

'I think they should be there,' I say, and wonder if I'm so sure about this because my father had taken me to his father's funeral. Grandpa: I can still remember his body in the Chapel of Rest—the waxy stillness, the room's stiff coldness, the plush firelit lining of the coffin. I can remember, too, my father's pious hush and muted upset. He said later he'd taken me there to show death was nothing to be frightened of, to reveal the un-terror of mortality, and perhaps he had half-succeeded: I'd been shaken, not scared. But I wouldn't be showing my children *his* body. They'd have to settle for a closed coffin in church.

'Funny the vicar saying he never met Dad,' my mother remarks later. 'He did, sort of. He'd only been here a week or so, but then he heard about my fall and came to the house.

Dad chatted to him a bit on the doorstep, not unpleasant or anything, but he wouldn't let him in, said I was too ill to see anybody. And of course, being Dad, he couldn't resist telling him that he didn't hold with church. Maybe that's why he's blotted it out, or was pretending to. I hope he doesn't try to get his own back on Friday.'

Coffin

SHE WILL SLEEP with him tonight. She worries that it's macabre, but I encourage her: she must do what feels right. And she says this is the last night she'll ever have him here, and she wants them to spend it together.

We are sitting on the bed round midnight, and she is stroking his hair and kneading his face and then she tweaks his nose and says: 'Icy. But you never did complain of the cold, did you?' We have kept the window open, which is just as well because we've not been able to turn the radiator off and from time to time I catch a whiff of something I don't much want to think about. His face, the chin propped up on its T, is still perfect. He has always been a great sleeper ('I was really hard on,' he'd say when he woke from an afternoon nap or evening pre-pub zizz), and all this sleeping he is doing now seems his apotheosis—the hardest sleep of all. 'No, the easiest,' says my mother when I try this conceit on her: 'No dreams, no worries about oversleeping, nothing.'

She leaves the room and I lift back the sheet. It isn't him in quite the same savoury way now. There is a deep blackberry bruise spreading either side of the stomach scar—the skin looks papery-thin and in danger of oozing or bursting. Little red lines have appeared on parts of his bleached hands. The back of his neck, from what I can make out, has gone purple and discoloured, all the blood gathering there. I admire her for sleeping with him, but hope she won't slip between the same sheets, that she'll find a way to fold them so that her warm flesh isn't up against his cold.

When I come in at seven next morning, she's breathing beside him. Later, when I return, I find she's been crying.

'I've just been talking to my little man.'

'What about?'

'Oh, I've been telling him he shouldn't have gone and left me alone like this—not so soon.'

'I'm sure he didn't want to.'

'No, I know, I don't mean to be nowty. But the fact remains: he's upped and gone.'

She berates him some more, and I think of Cleopatra berating Antony:

Hast thou no care of me, shall I abide
In this dull world, which in thy absence is
No better than a sty.

This is the way the world goes, the men running out on the women, running out *before* the women. A shorter life-expectancy: there's one great inequality men can brandish on their placards, can grumble about to women, who endure most of the others. But perhaps even in this women—as the ones left painfully behind while their husbands move beyond pain—end up suffering the most.

In the next room the phone goes again. Each time it rings, my mother has to confirm the rumour or accept the condolences and live his death over again. At least in here, by the bed, the phone is disconnected. I laugh with her about this— how we've not wanted the phone to ring and disturb his sleep, how no vacuuming has been done for the same reason, how we find ourselves whispering or low-voiced not out of grief and piety but because it would be such a pity to wake him. The GP has been fine about our holding on to the body—said that if we kept the room cold enough we could have him here right up to the funeral. We decided against that: he's going today; we don't want the house to be a morgue or chamber of rest, just to hang on to him a little longer, get used to him not being in his body.

'Do you think it's odd what we're doing?' I ask my mother. 'What's standard?'

'Remove the body and put it in a coffin on the day of death, I suppose.'

'This seems better.'

'When someone dies at home, anyway.'

'Even for those who die in hospital: you could bring them home.'

'I don't know—when people get maimed in accidents . . . '

'Maybe not them. But if someone drops dead in the street of a heart attack, and the relatives want him home, why shouldn't they get the body back, and sit with it?'

'It wouldn't be right for everyone.'

'But it's like the authorities fear for the corpse and won't let it out of their sight, as if it were going to get chopped up or boiled down or something.'

'No, it's just the palaver of organizing it.'

'The undertakers could do that. A day or two with the body at home could all be part of the service.'

We sit on, my mother and sister and I. At twelve-thirty we spend a last half-hour beside the bed. We don't say much, no grand finales or profundities, and when my mother leaves to go next door with my sister, not wanting to be present when the undertakers arrive, she simply kisses him on the

168

brow and says, 'Goodbye, my love.' I take the covers off for
one final, secret look at him. No secrets left himself, he lies
like an open book. The belly is more swollen now above the
fawn pyjama bottoms. Little blisters have formed around the
long stomach scar: his skin here is like ancient parchment,
crumbling once touched. His body begins to seem degraded
and demeaned in some way now—something which, even
when it was scavenged by disease, it had never done. 'You
have to look after yourself,' he had always said, and he had
done so until . . . Until when? Until a month ago, when an
unusually virulent or, well, *healthy* cancer had overcome him?
Until three months ago, when my mother's fall had kicked
that nice-and-slow cancer into life? A year ago, when he
began to complain of tiredness? Two years ago? There's no
saying when. There's only this moment, which happens to be
this moment, but which would feel this bad whenever it
happened. Now he is past looking after himself. Now he has
stopped. I shut the covers on him, the end of the story.

The undertaker's car pulls up outside the window, not a
hearse but a Ford Escort estate. The coffin looks to be made of
a sort of pale pine, like the bookshelves I've put up without
him. Malcolm, the boss, and the middle-aged assistant wearing
a carpenter's apron, have some difficulty manoeuvring the box
down the hall and into the room: 'Gently does it.' Finally they
put it down on the far side of the bed. The thinner end of the
coffin, for the feet, is hard up against the wardrobe. They chat
and dither, awkward about getting on with moving the body,
perhaps expecting me not to be here. They ask whether I
want little white drapes—see, like this, stapled against the
side—to conceal his pyjamas: they know no one is likely to
come and see him in the Chapel of Rest, but if anyone does
we won't mind if the coffin is open, will we, and these drapes
may be more discreet. They take the lid off to show me his

resting place: there is nothing plush about it, no purple velvet, no fancy panelling or inlay, just some white-cotton-lined foam under the head, plain and cheap as he'd have wanted. The phone goes, and they look at me, thinking this will be their chance to get the body in unobserved, but I keep jabbering and let it ring until it stops. I've been waiting for this moment, I'm not going to let him out of my sight.

Now Malcolm slips his arms under my father's shoulders, while his sidekick holds the ankles. They lift him clear of the bed, being careful not to knock his head against the bedside cabinet, where his clock and and brush-and-comb set and drinking glass with the hunting motif are still laid out. They hold him suspended above the coffin a moment, and try to ease him down—as if he were a living body needing careful handling, or me a relation needing careful handling: 'Gently does it.' But both the legs and head judder and jolt a bit as he hits the bottom of the coffin, sort of bounce or spring back unnaturally, no working muscles to absorb the strain, and I see the meaning of the phrase *dead weight*. It's taken till now, till that judder, for me to accept that he is dead, that he's vacated the premises of himself. They start to manoeuvre the lid on, with its name-plate 'ARTHUR B MORRISON Died 15 December 1991, Age 75 years', and I do not even try to see his face one last time: there's no need, it's not him. The lid clicks home.

They lift the wooden box, and get it out of the bedroom and back down the hall without destroying any of my mother's porcelain. At the door I hand the green cremation form over, and Malcolm says he's sorry the GP hasn't been up to remove the pacemaker: 'He'll do it at the chapel of rest: you won't mind not being there, will you? I'll make sure he keeps it for you.'

'OK.'

I watch the Escort pull away and feel angry with myself that I didn't insist on seeing the scalpelling out of the pacemaker. I wanted to know if I could take that. I wanted to stand there while his body was opened up, his skin slit open, and not faint or be squeamish or feel that wince in the stomach that the sight of blood brings. *Sang froid*: I wanted to prove that I possessed it, that I could be a doctor like him.

Back in the bedroom I find a large bloodstain on the sheet and bolster where his shoulders and head have been, where the blood had gathered once it was no longer pumped around. There must have been a small skin-tear there, a nick in the neck, from which it has seeped. I pull the sheet from the bed, the pillowcase from the bolster, and take them through to the washroom. I pick up an old dishcloth and wipe the blood and other fluids from the red plastic sheet that had covered the mattress. The body has gone but there is still a faint smell in the room, not unpleasant—a depersonalized decomposition may be part of it, but I can get his sweat and body-scent, too, the distinctive odour of him, engine oil and rosehips. I go back to the washroom, and let the cold water wash his blood away, let it stream to transparency under the tap, thinking how often I'd seen him with gashes on his fingers or purple-mooned fingernails, the wounds of carelessness, of saws and chisels lost hold of at crucial moments, or the day the top part of the extension ladder hurtled down and tore open his forehead and he stood unreacting there with a beck of crimson running into his eye. I pour myself a drink, gather up another box of photographs and sit on the empty bed. There he is, lying in an easy chair with a cat or dog in his lap, or with his arm round a good friend, or round the wife of a good friend. Often there is a drink in his hand; until the late sixties, when he bought his chalet down in Wales and gave up the habit, there is a cigarette, too. I wonder whether drink or smoking contributed to the cancer. I push my

171

fingers against my ribs to feel my heart, which is, so it seems to me, all over the place, a double or triple beat in every ten. He used to worry—no need now—that I would predecease him, and would bang on about me learning to look after myself better; I'd snap back that I was fine, and would he shut up, and that if anything was going to give me a coronary it was the stress of listening to him nag me. Once, not long ago, he had placed a stethoscope against his heart, then against mine, to test the difference: he had wanted, I think, not to show me how bad his health was, but to reassure himself how immortal I was. There is still a difference between us, but not the same one: we have both moved on a stage, he into the silence past all monitoring, I forced to listen to a strained, erratic heart. Patron and protector, he'd been the wall between me and death; now that wall is gone; now I'm on my own.

Pacemaker

A HOT AUGUST afternoon in my sister's garden: quiche and sandwiches, lager and wine, the milling of the extended family in and out of the kitchen, the lounge, the playroom. We are here after the christening of my sister's second child, Liam, now six months old. We are here, too, to celebrate the reprieved life of her first child, Louise, who about this time a year ago was lying unconscious on the side of the road in Spain—a car crash, the child thrown from her mother's arms in the back seat, a piece of skull pressing against her brain which somebody had the nouse to break off: Louise survived, she came home, she is here. The sun lies in stripes on the deck-chairs. Two dogs chase each other up the garden path. My father, beaming, takes his shirt off, as he likes to at the least excuse, but which he's not done lately in public. To me, who knows, there's no mistaking the give-away box shape high up on his ribcage.

His heart had become erratic; he'd begun to lie awake at nights, hearing rapid blips like the ones you got in old phone boxes when your money was running out. Now he has the dual chamber machine to control it. Before the operation he wrote to me, enclosing a leaflet from the British Heart Foundation

173

('*physiological* pacemakers require complex electronic circuitry and often need *more than one electrode lead*'—his underlining) and one of his own diagrams. The diagram showed a yellow line going from the pacemaker box into both the upper and lower chambers of the heart. Red lines denoted the main arteries, and there was a pink vertical one to show the central nervous system, with Christmas-tree branchings off it marking the (in his case faulty) nerve fibre. It looked like one of his old drawings of car engines, the sort he'd sketch when trying to make me grasp how pistons and carburettors and spark-plugs worked. It was hard to believe it was a drawing of him.

'It's shaken him, you know,' my mother says. 'It's hurt his pride—having to have an aid to get by.' Only the immediate family knows about the pacemaker: it mustn't get out that Arthur has a dicky heart, 'not till I snuff it.' But today he sits there chatting to neighbours and nieces, his chest bared in challenge. At a quiet moment he takes me to one side, jubilant: 'Not a bugger's twigged. Not a bugger's said a word. Maybe I'm not so decrepit after all.'

Early evening we go to the Cross Keys. For years it's been a sore point between us. He likes his seven o'clock pint, then back in time for dinner on the table at eight-thirty. I like a drink too, but why can't he stay at home and have one? I have small children to put to bed; I have a wife who'd rather be drinking with us than left behind; I belong to a generation which finds something a bit suspicious or unhealthy in these men-onlys. 'Home's not the same as the pub,' he says, putting his coat on, unwilling to break routine: 'Are you coming?' Sometimes I give in and join him, then spoil things for both of us with moroseness. But usually I resist and stay behind on principle, watching him go and feeling guilty—feeling envy, too, envy of his freedom from domesticity, his independence and separateness, which date back to the war. The tension in

174

such little things! So much between us! But tonight's a truce. Tonight we're relaxed and benign. Tonight I sit with him over his bitter, boys together in the huge, carpeted, knock-through lounge.

'Not like it used to be here,' he says, 'not like when Brian and Hilly had it.' There'd been a wall, once, where we are sitting: the lounge bar for the bourgeois on one side, the tap-room for the workers on the other. He usually opted for the latter, with its darts and benches and bare-board floor: 'That's where you find your decent, honest sort.' The taproom brought out the populist in him, the sentimentalist, the inverted snob: he preferred the company of farm-hands, plumbers and mechanics to the solicitors and mill-owners out front. Or so he claimed: what he liked, I suspected, was everyone in their proper place, and him able to move back and forth as he pleased, man of the people, doctor of the public house. The new democratic knock-through ruined that. He lost his special status. The pub became a classless mélange.

'No, not like it used to be,' he says. This is the downside of being seventy-one. The upside is a fund of memories which, when he's relaxed like this, he enjoys cracking open (a fund like the beer-stuck pillar of pennies that's gathering on the bar waiting for a local celebrity to knock it over). *Remember that time*, he leads off: when we all went to the Lakes on holiday, and bought four yellow Lakeland windcheaters, a quartet of clones, kitted out like golden orioles, the swish family Morrison. *Remember that time*, I respond, taking up the pace: when he tried out his new camera, the one with the delayed shutter action, and posed us on a steep hillside so that—on the 3D-less prints—we looked like an acrobat troupe standing on each other's heads. *Remember that time*: when we waved our Union Jacks at the Queen and her two children in Harrogate (older brother, younger sister, just like me and Gillian), or later,

175

snooping near Balmoral, pursued the royal hunting jeep along a moorland track. *Remember that time*: when we opened the village youth-club in our converted barn and people crowded in from as far away as Colne and Nelson. *Remember that time*: getting up at dawn to water-ski on a millpond of a sea, Abersoch at its best, the hop-start on the shoreline, then the carve and swish of the single fin in the water, the photos of us afterwards attempting turns so sharp our ears seem to brush the water. *Remember that time*: the three-month trip across Canada and the States in 1973, those thousands of miles, the bear that sniffed our tent in Yosemite, the salmon we wood-smoked on Vancouver Island, the man in Taos giving directions to an eating house called (we thought) The Petrified Chicken, on and on, New York, New Mexico, Houston, Toronto, the Dormobile papered over with stickers . . .

But I remember other times, less easy to speak of, or the same times, differently textured. That trip across North America? I'd had my girlfriend with me, too, the five of us hemmed in together, and I endured not only three months' tension and sexual frustration but a twenty-two-year-old's shame that I'd not yet got away from my parents. The youth club? Pep pills began to circulate more freely than in my father's surgery. And after nine, when the lights were dimmed for the disco, couples would snog in dark corners, and my father, the sex policeman, went round breaking them up. Abersoch? As well as water-skiing, there'd been the time, at seventeen, when I got drunk with two friends and, after the pub, carried home an armful of orange traffic-cones and red reflector plates. The police nabbed us at the camp-site, pushed us about, took our names and addresses. We thought we'd got off, but two months later the letter came: wilful damage, resisting arrest, larceny, appearance will be required in court in North Wales. It was the larceny that upset my father: 'You'll never get a decent job with that on your record.' He made us write abject letters to the Chief Superintendent. And when that didn't work, he got himself 'the best solicitor in the Lleyn Peninsula.' We drove down in the dead of winter, slate-grey rain, a courtroom with paraffin heaters. Our chief defence seemed to be the number of 'O' levels we had between us. The solicitor played the class card: 'These young men before you . . . grammar school boys on the brink of important careers . . . one moment of summer madness . . . ' We got fined a tenner each for the damage (my father paid), and were let off the rest. I ran across one of the policemen in the gents, who said, shamefaced, 'If we'd known what kind of lads you were . . . ' But it was me who felt shamefaced. Part of me hadn't wanted to be got off, had wanted us to be put in prison for a very long time.

I can't tell him this now. I can't tell him about the girls we met that same summer and how I so fell in love with mine that I said to my friend: 'If there'd been a firing squad last night, one life to be taken, hers or my father's, I'd have chosen his.' *Remember that time*: what, when I was callow, callous, ungrateful, disloyal, parricidal?

I walk over to the bar and buy us another drink and let his reminiscences wash over me. He's reached the near-present now, Louise's accident, the two-inch square of bone missing from her forehead, the skull cap she had to wear, the latest tests showing that the tissue behind the hole has begun to harden—when the light catches her brow, you can still see it throbbing. 'You never know,' he says, the roll and pulse of fruit machines behind him. 'One sharp instrument, even a stick, could still do it. Same with me: even with the pacemaker I could have a coronary. Your grandfather died at sixty-eight. I'm seventy-two next month. I feel I could go on till I'm ninety, but you just don't know.'

Not knowing, afraid that time is running out, I try to steer him on to Auntie Beaty. For years I'd wanted to arraign him, stand him, handcuffed, in front of me till his secret crimes had been exposed. I'd shout the charges so that all the court could hear them—lies, infidelity, cruelty to my mother—and ask him: How do you plead? Now it's different. Now I'm an adult. Now I don't pretend to judge. Now I see him in the mirror when I dress, feel myself becoming him, fear that I'm inheriting all the faults he would have wanted to save me from. I don't want to accuse, only get him to come clean with me. And then there'll be nothing between us. Then I will tell him I understand.

He comes back from the bar—a last bitter for him, Guinness for me.

'Remember the time we used to spend at the golf club?' I say.

'Great days, great days. I had a handicap of twelve then.'

'And the bar afterwards, with Auntie Beaty.'

'The nineteenth hole, and those onion and sugar sandwiches. Great times.'

'She meant a lot to you, Beaty, didn't she?'

'Great girl, great girl. Every weekend, Sam and little Josephine, too. I helped design their bar extension.'

'I know that, Dad, but you were crazy about Beaty, weren't you—in love with her, I mean.'

'Obsessed, maybe.'

'You used that word once before.'

'Did I?'

'At Abersoch, years ago—don't you remember? You were on at me about morals. I accused you of hypocrisy. I was way over the top, and brought Beaty up, and tried to get you to talk.'

'Maybe it's you who's obsessed.'

'Maybe. But come on. It was more than obsession with you.'

'More? I don't know. Don't see Beaty and Sam now. Moved away down south. Time we made a move ourselves, isn't it?'

Outside swallows are skimming the canal. The sun is sinking, and the moon is a pale thin wafer opposite, the ghost of its dead mother. He hands me the keys to his new Ford: 'The big thing is the power steering—see if you like how she handles.'

I head off up the A59, past the rectory where Canon Mackay used to live, the *other* rectory in the parish, the one the Church of England chose to keep, letting the one in Thornton go to us. 'What do you think?' my father asks. 'Picks up nicely, doesn't she.' At West Marton I turn left by the village shop, boarded up now: 'Nice, easy turning action, eh?' Two miles from home there's a little humpback bridge over the canal: when you take it fast, as my father used to, the heart lifts and empties as the wheels leave the ground. I try again. It feels like my last chance.

'You can tell me about Beaty, you know. I'm grown-up now. There needn't be any secrets.'

'Yes,' he says. Then after a pause, 'Great thing, power steering: never miss it till you've had it, but once you have you'll never go back to ordinary.'

Sandra

THE DAY BEFORE the cremation I drive my mother down to Earby, to see a man about funeral baked meats, and then on to the hairdresser. 'I'll be done in about an hour,' she says, and I push on towards Kelbrook, parking by a row of terraces. It was cobbled here once; the houses have bathrooms now, and satellite dishes, and pebble-dash. Sandra's is the last door on the right, navy blue. She appears in an apron, and with a duster in her hand. 'I thought you might come,' she says. 'I'm dusting.'

Sandra was Pat's predecessor, the maid before. She'd come from a broken home in Scotland in 1963. I was thirteen. She was nineteen. My sister had just gone away to boarding-school. We were alone a lot, sharing the same teenage stuff—*Titbits*, *Top of the Pops*. She was young for her age after the traumas back home, and my father had felt protective, treated her as a daughter as much as an employee, and was upset when she left. But she had a boyfriend by then, and found a cheap flat to rent, and had got a better-paid job on the till at a petrol station in Barnoldswick. She'd married the boyfriend but the marriage hadn't lasted—only the son had, grown up now. Sandra stayed close to my parents, always remembered birthdays and often called in. She felt grateful to them, for one thing: my father had lent her money to buy her house—this house where she's now pouring the tea out, and asking me how it was at the end, and saying: 'You won't mind if I dust round you, will you? My mam's coming down for Christmas, and if I don't do it now I never will.'

From a wooden stool she shakes a feather duster at the pot rail, the sideboard, the glass display case with her collection of thimbles and miniature dolls. She's wearing blue jeans and a red sweatshirt which rides up from the waist as she stretches—she's not lost her slimness, and her face is still attractive under the reddish hair, permed and frizzy now, not Twiggy-straight. My father's death, the flood of grief and nostalgia, my acute physical awareness of her have removed any barriers. Without meaning to, I've slipped into the old flirtatious banter we used when we were teenagers:

'Funny us being alone in a house again.'

'What do you mean?'

'You know what it used to mean.'

'Oh, I've given all that up: life seems less complicated without.'

'Don't you get lonely?'

'Not really.'

'But it's such a waste. How old are you now?'

'Forty-eight next month.'

'A terrible waste.'

'Nah.'

My parents had always had maids. Rosa, who was Austrian, had come in 1946 and stayed until 1958, when we moved the mile from Earby to Thornton: I could remember only a sweet-natured, hard-to-hear-properly granny figure who'd be ironing or making cakes while I lay with the labradors under the kitchen table, and who one day rushed in flour-faced from the

garden with a swarm of bees in her white hair. Then came
Lennie, in her late twenties, a beanpole with a long runny
nose, prone to moods and silences. She must have seen me
through from childhood to puberty—I can remember walking
into her bedroom in my underpants, a twelve-year-old
swooning in self-regard at an erection (she saw me off by not
noticing). When she married a carpenter called Jeff, and they
emigrated to Australia, there followed a dismal brief succession
of housekeepers: the one who cooked us mixed grills, spent all
evening crying in her room and left after three weeks; another
who left after twenty-four hours; a third who might have lasted
longer but who walked into the bathroom one morning when
my father was (his phrase) 'on the throne' and blithely continued cleaning around him—even he found that a bit too
informal. Sandra was a desperate last shot, immature but sweet-
natured. She had stayed two years; and even when she'd left,
and Pat had taken over, she'd never really gone away.

A pretty nineteen-year-old in a big house in a strange place
far from home might have felt bored and unattended, especially
since the job was so undemanding: I was at school all day, my
sister at home only in the holidays, my parents unfussy about
cleaning but needing someone to cook occasionally and answer
the phone while they were out on their visits. But if Sandra
was lonely she never showed it. Soon tradesmen and farm-
hands and older schoolfriends of mine and any male with the
remotest excuse to call were paying court, and she happily
flirting back. The kitchen with its Aga was the centre for this
and most other activities in our house. I'd perch there on my
stool under the window, pretending to do homework in
thrilling proximity to the world of would-be adult sex, when
only a year before, at twelve, the mechanics of intercourse (as
relayed to me by a friend at grammar school) had seemed so
incredible and disgusting that I'd refused to believe them. My

parents, being doctors, might have been expected to fill me in about sex, but by the time my father finally broached the facts of life with me as I lay in bed one morning, both of us deeply embarrassed, I had already lost my virginity.

It was a boyfriend of Sandra's called Steve who brought the world of sex even closer. Steve was in his last year at grammar school and so a year younger than her. But he was swanky and handsome and tough—once, at the local swimming-pool, I suspect egged on by me, he had started trying to beat up two 'posh little boarding-school cunts' and got us ejected and banned. Sandra, impressed, lighted on him among her other suitors, and they began going out together, though going out seemed to mean staying in and drinking coffee by the Aga. His banter grew in confidence until it reached a sort of Mellors-like bluntness (I was just discovering Mellors, too: my mother must have bought her copy of *Lady Chatterley's Lover* shortly after the trial: she kept it in her bedside cupboard, and I furtively took it off to bed whenever she was out). I wondered whether much of Steve's banter wasn't for my sake—a piece of machismo more to impress the jealous schoolboy with his homework than to seduce the maiden.

'Tha's got a nice pair.'

'Shut up' (flicking a duster at him).

'Gi' us a feel.' He'd lunge, she'd push him off. 'Go on, Blake wants one too, dunt tha?'

I did, and—emboldened by Steve's bluntness—in his absence sometimes tried for one, my mother once walking in on us as we wrestled near the dining-room cupboard and disguised our sexual tussle as a fight to get out the carving knife for supper. Then, one night when my parents were out and Steve not there either, after a long session of innuendo, Sandra emerged from her room wearing a new bikini: 'How do I look?' I'm not sure what she expected, but for me, seeing her vulnerable but also pleased with herself, this was the chance at last to touch her breasts. I came at her. She fought me off. We fell to the floor. I tried to undo the bikini top, failed, got my hand inside it, slid on, down towards the elastic of her bikini pants. She fought harder now, squirming and panicking—it had got out of hand, wasn't supposed to go this far, but now I felt the brush of pubic hair and suddenly, cornily, miraculously, like some bad old film cliché, we stopped fighting and began kissing. On the bed, she told me to be *careful*. There was no need. In a few seconds, the moment she touched me, I came.

I didn't know what to expect—anger and remorse, probably. But next morning, my parents out again, I went to her while she was hoovering, and we walked wordlessly upstairs. Neither of us quite understood what was happening: it was innocent, clitoral, barely-penetrative sex, though that morning I ruptured the little thread at the back of my foreskin: there was blood all over the place, but it was me whose hymen had been broken, not her. She told me later that she had lost her virginity to a friend of her father's when she was fifteen— her only time. She never did sleep with Steve.

We went on having sex for six months, a year, till she found a proper boyfriend and left. It was usually on Friday evenings during term-time, when no one else was in the house, though we took our chances when we could. We'd be up in her bedroom, under the open window, listening for the sound of my parents' car coming up the drive, the door slamming in the yard or the key in the front door. And this meant it was a detached, alert, silent kind of lovemaking, one ear open above the swoosh of the flesh. We were both terrified of my father walking in on us.

'It's all a long time ago,' she says, moving her stool under another stretch of pot rail.

'Yes, we were more or less kids.'

'The last time was after that friend of yours was killed.'

'Nick Proctor, you mean.'

He had died in a car crash one Christmas, some time after Sandra had gone. Four of them had been on their way to a party I'd told them about in Barnoldswick—Brian Smith and his cousin Bernie in the front, Bob Skelton and Nick in the back. The Rover they hit on a bend at Broughton sent the back of their Mini into a low wall with trees behind it. My father, drinking in the local pub, The Bull, was early on the scene. Brian led him to where the bodies lay among elm and drystone and metal, Bob already dead, Nick clearly dying. At Airedale Brian met me histrionically: 'Look at these hands—that's Nick's blood.'

'I remember,' I say. 'I stopped off on my way back from the hospital.'

'Bit of a risk. I'd broken up with Mick by then, but he sometimes came round when he was drunk. And there was the baby.'

'I was upset. I realized you weren't keen. It was a bit like this—a death.'

'Wanting comfort, yes, I understand that. But I've given up, I told you.'

'If you change your mind . . .'

My father had found out of course, after a bit, I'm not sure how. He met me off the school bus, and was oddly understanding: we were young, we'd been alone in the house, it was innocent and natural, he wasn't going to tell Mummy. But what we had done was also very wrong: we must *never never* do it again or he would have to kick me out. If I'd been more mature I would have seen he couldn't have meant the last bit: the obvious solution to this teenage sex problem would have been to dismiss Sandra, not expel me. But he didn't do that either: she, too, was given a (rather heavier) lecture and

185

allowed to stay. Later, looking back, I thought it to his credit that he hadn't done the expected middle-class thing and sacked her (it was me who had done the expected middle-class thing and fucked her). Perhaps, too, I wasn't so scared by him as I thought I was: within weeks, we resumed.

But sex after that always seemed a thing to be done furtively and silently: terrible retribution might be walking up the stairs. In my callow, febrile way I wondered if my father and Sandra might be doing it too: that would explain why he hadn't given her the push—so as to carry on, or not risk her exposing him. But she denied this, and in the end, when I understood their relationship better, I believed her: she was more surrogate daughter than surrogate wife. Less easily suppressed was the suspicion that he took a vicarious thrill in trying to catch us out. One night, in bed with Sandra, I heard the tiniest click of the key in the front door and fled naked to my room. He crept up the stairs and walked straight into her bedroom, where he found her sitting, just a towel round her waist, at the dressing-table. She covered herself and was indignant: what did he mean walking in without knocking? He came into my room, where I feigned sleep. There was nothing he could prove.

I never talked to him, later, about what had happened, but I can imagine his pragmatic way of shrugging it off: 'Leave two men together in a room for long enough and they'll kill each other. Leave a man and woman alone together in a room for long enough and they'll screw each other. No way round it—law of nature. There are worse things in life than what you two did.'

'You forget,' I say to Sandra, leaning against the door-frame while she dusts on, 'You were my first love. You predate everyone.'

'Hum. I suppose.'

'It never felt wrong.'

'Not for you maybe.'

'It still doesn't.'

'You don't give up, do you—you think you're different but you're just like all the other fellas. Tell you what: how about making us another cuppa?'

I leave the room, and put the kettle on, half-ashamed of my flirtatiousness, needing the escape and obliteration of sex, but hating the hard little bit of myself I've just been hearing, so manipulative and opportunistic. Is it unnatural to want her now? Or would it be unnatural not to?

'Here you are,' I say, putting a mug of tea down by her feet on the stool, 'I'll have to go. My mother will be waiting.' And she is, with her funeral hairdo.

That night I dream Sandra comes to my bed. She drives up to Thornton, lets herself in with her old Union, and silently climbs the stairs. 'Here's that tea,' she says, and when she puts it down I see the glass half-pint tankard my father took his last sip from. It's five in the morning and I'm wodgy with sleep, but not so much that I can't work out why she is here. She is wearing a baby-doll nightdress from the mid sixties and I try to pull her into bed. She resists at first, changing her mind or preserving her dignity, but soon she lies beside me on the blankets, then under them. I touch her breasts, her neck, her navel—a nineteen-year-old's. Even the noiselessness is the same, the stroking-more-than-kissing, the ear open for trouble —for what if my mother should wake? Sandra is worried, too, I can tell. I come at once, the premature ejaculator of fourteen.

'Better go,' she whispers into my head.

'Sorry, I wanted it to be longer, I wanted to do it properly.'

The dream seems to be over then, because I'm downstairs in the kitchen and can feel the teapot cooling on the Aga. But the tankard in my hand is full of blood, not tea, and I swill it away, rinsing the glass to transparency. I must find my father, I think, but my mother is in bed alone, deeply asleep, a Dick Francis novel face down on the floor, her arm hanging out as if to retrieve it. Upstairs again, I check the door to my room (closed), then to Pat's room (locked), and come to the spare room, which is open.

'You're still here,' I say.

'I was always here. It was you who left,' says Sandra.

I close the door behind me, and get into her bed and into her. It is the same long dream of memory, but better this time, wetter, less awkward, no guilt. We hang on to each other, rocking the cradle of childhood together, calling back the old days, wanting to hear his car on the tarmac, his key in the front door, his footstep on the stairs. We're noisy now, to wake him, we push and rock and come, but my father does not come, will never hear us now, though we hold each other in his memory, in the daze of his loss, hoping beyond hope that now, finally, he will walk in on us.

Funeral

HAIL AND FAREWELL. Snow on Pendle. Gales. Storms. A great sweeping coldness. The Aire has flooded its banks from Skipton through to Otley. In the hurled elms the rooks' nests look like blood-clots, not about to be shifted.

The *Craven Herald* has a fame beyond Skipton because it's one of the last newspapers in the country to devote its front page entirely to advertisements. Here they all are. Skipton Auction Mart announces the sale of 722 store and breeding sheep, 600 store and suckler cattle with young bulls, 209 in-calf dairy cows and heifers, 23 young feeding bulls, 250 gritstone ewes and shearlings, 127 hogs, 5 rams, 1 Lim X heifer with calf at foot. In the Soroptimist Rooms, Skipton Bookmen have a discussion by D. Price of *Great Expectations*. The Plaza is showing *Home Alone*. There are jumble sales, civic balls, car boot sales, barn dances, coach excursions for Christmas shopping at the Gateshead Centre, carol services, parties and bazaars. North Yorkshire County Council confirms the order to divert the bridleway from grid reference SD 8329 5509 south east to a new route at the C393. The Personal column offers clairvoyance and tea-leaf readings and bunny kissograms.

When the last-but-one editor, barely thirty, took over the *Craven Herald*, there was speculation that he'd end the tradition of these front page ads. But he'd barely had chance to settle into the job when he died in a potholing accident up in Malham. The current editor is sixtyish, an old friend of my father's, and not about to change anything.

I'd feared what he would write in his obituary. When he came the other day he didn't seem much interested in the shilling-life facts we had prepared for him; indeed we barely got a word in between his orotundities. 'It is so gracious of you to receive me in such a time of distress—would that it had been in happier circumstances.' 'Let it not be said that Arthur was a retiring man, for all that he had retired: some would say that, *au contraire*, he verged on the interventionist, nay even bullying.' It seemed odd hearing this Latinate purple coming from a red-faced Yorkshireman, and I wondered whether it wasn't meant for me, or in parody of me—the boy who'd gone off to London and written books. But I underestimated him: among the stories of repossessions and GBH, today's paper carries a long piece, boxed off and brought forward from the obituaries page, informed by deep affection. The *Barnoldswick and Earby Times*, by contrast, has set a cub reporter on the job, who attributes my father's pugnacious village spirit to his 'RAF background' and makes him sound like a militaristic busybody. But perhaps I'm bad-tempered because this paper makes its front page lead not my father (who is down below the centre-fold) but a woman celebrating her hundredth birthday, smilingly marking up a quarter century he never had. I feel the same looking at the obituaries in the *Yorkshire Post*: my poor dead father, a spring chicken among columns of octo- and nonegenarians. At least no one could mistake that he is dead: everybody else has merely *passed on* or *fallen asleep*.

The hail begins to turn to snow. At my mother's behest, I

go through my father's wardrobe, his drawers, his bedside cabinet, in search of things I'd like to keep. It's a scene I've always dreaded, the great elegiac moment of coming into my father's clothes, but I've been through too many dress rehearsals for it to hurt, and not just in my head: ever since he retired my father has been handing down his shirts, his shoes, his money—'You can't take them with you,' he'd say. So I would rummage about, trying not to show how badly I wanted to wear some of the things he'd worn when I was a child—his 1947 white cotton tennis shirt with his name-tag sewn in red on the collar; his bomber jacket, his velvet waistcoat, his flat golf cap, his black-and-white spotted silk scarf, his Tootal and Kendal Milne ties. 'Are you sure you don't want this . . . ?' I'd say. 'Go on, take it, I've not worn that for years.' But now that he's gone, I feel like a grave-robber. I take three jumpers, a dozen pairs of socks, two pairs of brown leather shoes, some cuff-links, and stash them in an old RAF travel-bag of his. Then I put on his white nylon shirt, black tie, grey suit, black woollen socks, black shoes. I am going to his funeral in his clothes.

Back in the living-room, the snow is creeping up the double-glazed doors. Every minute it rises a little further, a wind-drawn tide of nothingness. Who will brave the roads in this? There are friends and relations due to come over the Pennines—will they get through? All the while the wind gets stronger, the snow thicker, and the hills my father built this house to look out on can no longer be seen. My sister arrives with her children and husband, who says: 'We might have known he'd choose a day like this, gales and hail and every bloody thing. I bet he's up there, pulling the strings, having a good laugh.'

At twelve the two funeral cars come, the hearse waiting at the bottom of the drive. We are not due at church, two minutes' drive away, till twelve-fifteen. Malcolm, the boss, drives up in a fourth car, his Escort estate. He comes to fetch us from the front door, and takes me aside a moment to hand over the pacemaker scalpelled from my father's chest. It is the weight and size and shape of a stopwatch. I turn it over to find the clock-face and, when no one's looking, hold it to my ear to listen for ticking. I clutch the pleasant plasticity of its sides, as if it were a precious stone—the talisman of my old man. I put it in my trouser pocket to fondle through the funeral, not letting go.

There is a wide tarmac area in front of the house, room enough in normal conditions for the two big black death limos to turn around, but in the ice and snow the manoeuvre is causing them trouble. Finally the cars are pointing in the right direction and—not rushing, not wanting to arrive early—we climb in. The front car moves towards the corner by the garage to turn off the forecourt into the drive. The capped chauffeur has not left himself much room. At the corner, between the drive and the garage, is a small path, edged with kerbstones, which deepens as it goes. When the front wheel crosses this it slithers down. The chauffeur stops, then revs and plunges forward to retrieve the damage, but only forces the front of the car deep and insurmountably down the path. He reverses, but he does not retreat far enough, and when he moves forward again, engine revving, he makes the same mistake. This time the back end of the car has slewed round and is no more than three inches from the garage wall.

We get out and have a look. It's agreed we should stay out—our weight may be making things more difficult. It is now twelve-fifteen. The chauffeur is looking flustered, removing his cap—its chiselled line in the sweat of his hair. Four of us get our hands under the rear bumper and bounce the car further from the wall, laughing as we do so. My brother-in-law slides a fallen tile under the rear nearside wheel. The chauffeur climbs back into the driving seat, reverses over the tile and back about three feet, then drives forward with steady intent, no high revs. The result is the same, or slightly worse: front end down the gutter, back end slewed an inch from the wall.

By twelve-twenty, we're resigned to the side of the car being damaged; only Malcolm is not. He stands there in the icy wind, fondling his chin, watching his profit margin being wiped out. Expenses: coffin/carpentry 500 pounds; hire of chauffeurs/pallbearers 200 pounds; cost to client 1,100 pounds; profit 400 pounds. A 500-pound repair on the Bentley would see that off. I can see his mind ticking over like a taxi meter, two sorts of panic wrestling in him—humiliation at getting the client late to the church, desperation not to let his car be scratched.

Now my brother-in-law remembers the pile of sand my father has accumulated nearby—a sandpit for the grand-children it was going to be. He gets a spade and scatters the sand under the rear wheels of the car, the path, the drive, the forecourt. We bounce the car clear of the wall, as before, and this time the chauffeur backs slowly over the broken tile and sand, gives himself a long run and negotiates the corner safely. It is twelve twenty-five.

We climb in again and join the hearse down at the bottom of the drive. 'I always used to tell him: you'll be late for your own funeral,' my mother says.

She's been distracted, like the rest of us, by the thought of people in church sitting and freezing and wondering what's gone wrong. But now there's no ignoring the coffin in the hearse just ahead of us and her top lip trembles. We need not have worried about a poor turnout. It's a quarter of a mile to the church, but before we're halfway there we see the cars parked on either side of the road. And as we pull in by the church gate, three spaces reserved for us, we see the cars stretching on towards Barnoldswick. We huddle in the wall by the church gate, hailstones slanting past, slashing slow snow, my mother pulling her black fur coat more tightly over her black cotton jacket.

Four pallbearers slide the coffin out and up on to their shoulders. There is a standard-bearer, too, a guard of honour from the British Legion: my father was president of the Earby branch for thirty-five years, and this man has been sent to walk immediately ahead of the coffin while my mother, my sister and I walk immediately behind. As we move inside the church I have an impression of large numbers, of rows and rows of heads as far as you can see. I stare down at the stone flags, their familiar cracks and stains. One Christmas I stood here and sang the first verse of 'Once in Royal David's City', suspecting that the mantle of soloist had fallen on me (like captaincy of the village cricket team, like the local reporter's weekly attention to my soccer performances) not out of any merit but because I was the doctor's son, or doctors' son.

Now the doctors' son, or doctor's son, is following the doctor up the aisle, for the first and last time. We step in time, my sister and I, she on my mother's left arm, I on the right, and just before we reach the front pew I risk lifting my face between the backs of necks and see ahead Heather and Amanda, the wives of my two cousins, weeping in the choir-stalls: this is for them that moment when you see the coffin and think of the body inside and the word 'dead' sinks home. We shuffle into the cold pew, and the first hymn starts up, 'O God Our Help in Ages Past'—my choice, though I'm wondering now about its aptness, the bleakness of its vision of human ephemerality: 'They fly, forgotten as a dream/Dies at the opening day,' we sing, but didn't our wreath say: 'We will never forget you'? I lift my head again, and see my cousins' wives still crying, and hear my daughter and her cousin in the row behind start to cry. 'Time like an ever-rolling stream/ bears all its sons away' makes me think of the moment during cremation when the curtains close and the coffin rolls away.

Now we are sitting. A neighbour from across the road is reading the lesson, from *The Pilgrim's Progress*. He has chosen this, he explains, because my father seemed to have something of a pilgrim about him, a man of communal spirit, one sometimes inclined to bully his fellow-men into making greater efforts, a cross between Mr Valiant-for-Truth and Mr Standfast: 'When the day that he must go was come many accompanied him to the River side, into which, as he went, he said, "*Death, where is thy sting?*" And as he went down deeper, he said, "*Grave where is thy victory?*" So he passed over, and trumps sounded for him on the other side.' My father would be sniggering at the 'trumps'. It was his word for fart. His trumps had filled my childhood as noisily as his snores.

We go to the second hymn now, 'Lead, Kindly Light', my mother's choice—there are those lines about 'encircling gloom', and the second stanza (surely she didn't intend this) brings back my father's stubbornness: 'I loved to choose . . . Pride ruled my will.' Sitting down again, I see the snow behind the stained-glass window of Moses parting the Red Sea. I imagine my father going under the waves, or under the sea, and I hear out there or in my head a quote from Ecclesiasticus:

And some there be, which have no memorial;
Who are perished, as though they had never been;
And are become as though they had never been born;
And their children after them.

The vicar begins to talk—knowledgeably: you wouldn't guess he didn't know my father. The congregation is like a great wave pressing at my back.

'The sermon I gave last Sunday, the day on which Arthur Morrison died, contained this phrase: "Some may think they have believed in Christ, though their life denied it. Others may not imagine themselves to have believed, though their life has affirmed it." It must be readily admitted that Arthur Morrison found little time for the Church and organized religion. He regarded *religious activity* as almost a contradiction in terms. He hated the time-wasting tedium of the committee. His whole life seemed to echo St James's words in his epistle: "Be doers of the word and not hearers only."

'Today we come to bid farewell to a loving husband and devoted father; a valued colleague in his medical profession; a caring counsellor and confidant; a good friend to high and low, rich and poor. The splendid Village Institute stands as a memorial to his vision and energy. But there were other examples: the successful youth club he ran in his stables' harness room; the Best Kept Village and Britain in Bloom competition successes; the car boot sales and endless raffles. We gather up these deeds and bring them before Almighty God.'

I half-turn, but the faces I see are all lifted to the vicar or sunk in memory of the car boot sales and Britain in Bloom. I feel time running fast through us all, and regret no one has brought a camera or camcorder, so we can play today back, so there can be a memorial. People video weddings—why not funerals, too?

The vicar is winding up: 'St Paul had a constant companion on his journeys across Asia Minor and into Europe: St Luke, whom Paul described as "the beloved physician"—on account of the love both given to and received from his patients. That phrase, "the beloved physician", sums up Arthur Morrison perfectly. May he rest in peace.'

We kneel with our psalters on blue-embroidered cushions, whispering to the children not to touch the large central heating pipe, black and hot beneath the pews. The last hymn, 'Jerusalem', isn't in Thornton-in-Craven's hymn-book; even in *The English Hymnal*, it creeps in only among the litanies, 656A, an annex to another hymn; we've had to get a sheet specially printed. My sister loves the music (she is crying before the first bar is over), and may have her other reasons: its fighting spirit; the 'dark satanic mills' that could be Earby's; and because it's by Blake, and my father's middle name (his mother's maiden name) is Blakemore—though he surely never read the poet in his life, would not have known who William Blake was if the name had come up in Trivial Pursuit.

Now the last prayers are over, and we stand to leave our pews, and the bearers are picking up the coffin. As the British Legion man walks ahead out of the choir-stalls the top of his pole catches the carved wooden screen, and for a long horrible moment it snags there. He retreats a step and waggles it, and still it won't come loose, but then he tries again, less discreetly, and it is free, and we turn behind him into the aisle, my mother, my sister and I in line together. I want to lift my head to nod meaningfully at the faces we now face, as if to say: It is all right, we are grieving but appeased now, thank you for coming. But I keep my head down until we are out of the porch and on to the wet flags and think: Now I will never know who was in church. The snow blows past, and I feel, belatedly, and with a sort of queasiness at feeling such feelings at all, the sort of pride my father once felt in me. His life had not flowered unseen, or been wasted on the desert air: the numbers proved it—here was a man of substance.

The crematorium is six miles away and it's a slow route. I imagine the funeral procession as the line of boys walking behind the teacher on a school outing in Truffaut's *Les Quatre*

Cent Coups—at each street corner someone slips away until only sir is left. The snow has stopped by the time we get there, but the wind is icier, and we wait in wreaths of breath while the coffin is unloaded again.

It is a short service: two minutes of Albinoni on tape (his Adagio in G Minor, a piece I'd taken to playing with doomy repetitiveness just before my father's illness), then the tape fading for three minutes of the vicar. As he speaks of committing to God this beloved servant, he reaches for the rope-pull which will swish the curtains round the coffin and activate the conveyor-belt—at which point Malcolm leaps from the front stalls and whisperingly intervenes: the family wish the coffin to remain visible and in place until after the service; it is they who will disappear, not the deceased. The vicar nods, the service ends, Albinoni resumes. We file out, a last look back at the big wooden box with the flowers on: it has so little to do with him, yet he is lying in it. As we reach the door, half a dozen mourners push through, late for this ceremony or early for the next. Outside, more cars pull up—one with my cousins in, who have lost their way. We stand for a moment or two in the knife of the wind. People shake hands with us, sorry for our trouble.

Down the side of the crematorium, by the little wooden makeshift cross marked A B MORRISON, are the wreaths: my mother's, the children's, the grandchildren's. I stand in his clothes—how well they fit me now—gazing down at the earth. Snow blows across his black scuffed shoes, the bottom of his greatcoat, his trouser turn-ups. Whoever put his cross up must have had trouble knocking the stake through the soil's icy heart. A tear of catarrh drops from the end of my nose. I dig my heel in but the ground won't give. I feel the frozen earth coming up through my soles.

★

We have put a white cloth over a table in his study, and this is where the bar is. I've arranged it, as he used to, in descending order of alcoholic strength: the serious bottles of brandy, whisky, rum and gin to the right; down through the sweet-sickly shades of vermouth, sherry and wine; on to the cellar-brown gleam of pale ales, Guinness and bitter; finally, far left, the bright, feel-good cartons of fruit juice. To one side of the bar, in front of his desk, its drop-lid firmly shut, is a lower, smaller table where the glasses and tankards are. He had a range of these: the dimpled pewter RAF tankard; the silver golf club mug, with its humanizing dent just below the twirly engraving; and countless other presentation cups—silver, brass, glass—won at squash or golf tournaments, or given at Christmas, one or two of which must still be hanging for him on hooks in local pubs. Among the glasses, in bowls, are crinkly crisps and salted nuts. Down the corridor, in the kitchen, are squishy, lard-tasting prawn vol-au-vents; ham and egg quiche; cheese and crab paste in thin-sliced, freckled brown sandwiches; old-fashioned Lancashire meat pies, yellow-crusted and serrated, and with a small jellied hole at the centre.

The mourners step into the house, rubbing their cold hands, stamping the snow from their shoes. They stand with drinks and cigarettes, and there's a strange euphoria about it, the release of afterwards and the illusion that the man we have come in memory of must be about the place, somewhere. Once there'd been a party like this every New Year's Eve, a Jacob's joint—the host supplying drink and everyone else contributing a cold dish or salad or dessert. The guests were always the same thirty or forty people, and the venues had varied at first, but in time it came down to my father to organize things, and—being an eager host and reluctant guest —this meant holding it at his home. In time, too, the numbers dropped: last year there'd only been twenty. This year there won't be a party at all—here it is, ten days early.

I move among the wake, offering drinks, receiving condolences. People have their memories: they pass them on (and I flesh them out). Jack Jones, from down the village, remembers coming back here one summer midnight two decades ago and walking round the rough paddock (whisky glasses in hand, a heavy dew), my father complaining of the lack of village spirit and outlining his plans to start a Men of Thornton evening, a monthly gathering in the bar of the Manor House Hotel. Uncle Ron remembers lying on his back in the November wind under my father's chalet, the two of them wirebrushing the sub-frame (the rust of sea salt, a drizzle of orange flakes). Brian and Hilly Thackeray remember staying in that same chalet one teenage summer, a crowd of us swimming in the dark (the lighthouse, phosphorescence, an angry man poking his head through the bedroom window after midnight demanding his daughter). Cousin Kela remembers the lobster my father caught by Llanbedrog headland; she had been sent back to fetch a bucket while the men used sticks to keep it from escaping (plunged grey in the boiling saucepan, it screamed and came out pink). Auntie Edna remembers how old Harry Hall took my father to court for refusing to chop the branches which hung over and took the light from his little cottage (a man in brown, suddenly frail and hard of hearing, winning the magistrate's sympathy; my father to comply, lop and pay costs). Cousin Richard remembers my father inviting him over from Manchester during the school holidays to chop dead trees for firewood at one-and-six an hour: he filled the stable with chunks of elm (faint ripple rings on their white sawn surfaces, rosettes of fungus on the side), and went home a rich man. Perhaps he also remembers (but it's not the day to mention it) my father forcing him to eat up his Brussel's sprouts one Christmas dinner (turkey, paper hats, the heat-blown fairies in the wire candle-holder tinkling round and round). And Auntie Beaty, who's here too of course . . . only Beaty's memories stay closed.

I keep the drinks topped up, his old job, ignoring the protests. The party has its own momentum now—wake or wedding, in the drink and cigarette smoke it's easy to forget which, easy to think it's just another New Year's Eve. But then I catch sight of my father's leather dog-lead hanging on the back of the door, and I think not just of him but of the others who aren't here, either—those whose deaths had made him morbid in his last decade. No Granny. No Auntie Mary. No Florrie Wallbank, with her beauty spots and her hair piled high in a swirl of silver (died of cancer). No Bobby Dickinson, diminutive in his yellow V-necked golf jumper and a handicap of eight (routine operation that went wrong, haemorrhage). No Uncle Charles staring from his violet pock-marked face (leukaemia), nor Auntie Selene, with her kind magistrate's eyes and dead, pasty, like-kissing-baking-powder cheeks (she had come six months after Charles's death complaining of stomach pains, and when my mother laid her down on the bed she could feel tumours as big as golf balls). No Joan O'Neill, with the hollowed horse face, my mother's great confidante, who lost two husbands from brain tumours before her own stroke. No Billy Cartwright, with his soft, doggy civility (keeled over from a heart attack while mowing the lawn). Above all, no Uncle Stephen, my godfather, who epitomized the exuberant unthinkingness—golf, alcohol and practical jokes—of my father's crowd. A year ago, home from the hospital where he was being treated for depression (Stephen? *depression?*), he had trooped down the garden to light a bonfire and was found in flames next to his petrol can; the inquest returned an open verdict. Fun and fresh air and cock-eyed optimism: it had all gone, with Stephen. Now my father had gone too.

As the light darkens, everyone prepares to leave, putting down paper plates and empty glasses, hunting for coats. We kiss or shake hands at the door: 'See you again,' I say, but when will the next time be—my mother's funeral, their own funerals? You have a childhood, and move away, and think vaguely that if you choose to come home again it will still be there, intact, as you left it. What was left of my childhood were these frail widows and widowers, stepping out into the snow, the coming night.

Back inside, on the living-room floor, among the wine spills and dropped crisps, my daughter and her cousin are sitting with paper and crayons. They have an uncanny intimacy for children who live two hundred miles apart and who hardly ever see each other—perhaps not uncanny since they were born on the same day within hours of each other, a co-incidence which became one of my father's great triumphs ('How often does that happen—two grandchildren at opposite ends of the country, born on the same day?'). Now they are seven. Their arms twined, their legs tucked under them, they have drawn a boat and written a story. They hand it to me, eighteen words long: 'When a ship gets poorly it goes to port. Then it dies, then it dies, then it dies.'

And when did you last?

When did you last see your father? Was it when they burnt the coffin? Put the lid on it? When he exhaled his last breath? When he last sat up and said something? When he last recognized me? When he last smiled? When he last did something for himself unaided? When he last felt healthy? When he last thought he might be healthy, before they brought the news? The weeks before he left us, or life left him, were a series of depletions; each day we thought 'he can't get less like himself than this,' and each day he did. I keep trying to find the last moment when he was still unmistakably there, in the fullness of his being, *him.*

When did you last see your father? I sit at my desk in the mortuary-cold basement of the new house, the one he helped me buy, his pacemaker in an alcove above my word processor, and the shelves of books have no more meaning than to remind me: these are the first shelves I ever put up without him. I try to write, but there is only one subject, him. I watch the news: Yugoslavia, the General Election, the royal separations—the news he didn't live to see. I've lost sight not only of his life, what it meant and added up to, but of mine. When my three children come back from school, their cries echo emptily round the house and I feel I'm giving no more than a stranger could give them—drinks, attention, bedtime stories. Never to have loved seems best: love means two people getting too close; it means people wanting to be with each other all the time, and then one of them dying and leaving the other bereft. A fox comes trotting up the lawn towards my window, printing itself in the dew, as though it owned the place. I feel as if an iron plate had come down through the middle of me, as if I were locked inside the blackness of myself. I thought that to see my father dying might remove my fear of death, and so it did. I hadn't reckoned on its making death seem preferable to life.

When did you last see your father? I try to remember where I first heard the question asked, or saw it written. I invent contexts for it: sprawled by their Harley Davidsons in some sixties film, their dope smoked, their six-pack emptied, late at night, two drop-out bikers have begun to confide in each other about their pasts, and one asks the other: 'When did you last see your father?' Another film, a television documentary about the young homeless, and in the horrid brightness of a police interview room a kindly WPC is eking what information she can from a fourteen-year-old Geordie boy found bruised and shivering in a shop doorway near King's Cross: 'When did you last see your father?' Or maybe it was my own father who had used the phrase. I remember him telling me, at some point in my late teens or twenties when I was drifting away from him, seeing less of him, how badly he'd taken the death of his father, and how he didn't want this to happen to me: 'I used to see Grandpa every weekend. But for some reason I'd not seen him for about six weeks, and then he had his heart attack and was dead. There were rows we'd had we hadn't really settled. I remember someone at the wake asking "When did you last see your father?" and me feeling terrible.' The absent patriarch, the orphaned child: there's no end of possibilities, no end of plots to this one story.

When did you last see your father? A friend says: 'You know it's a painting, of course. Something to do with Charles the Second, I think. It hung on the stairs in my boarding-school, the first thing you'd see each term, just what you needed when your father had dumped you like a sack of potatoes. You know the one—it's incredibly famous.' I don't know it, or if I do I've forgotten. But suddenly everybody I meet seems to allude to it, or parody the phrase: variations on it are the stuff of sitcoms or Whitehall farce. I turn up the painting shortly afterwards, a Victorian tableau of the Civil War, the Cavalier boy standing stiffly on a stool before a table of Puritan inquisitors—'And When Did You Last See Your Father?' I suppose I must have seen the painting before, but if so I'd forgotten it. Certainly I'd forgotten the 'And' in the title. Everyone else seems to forget it too, just as they forget the artist (W. F. Yeames) and mistake the subject (not Charles the Second, just a boy from any Royalist family). But the 'And' is important. It lets us know how cunning the interrogator is, how uncasual his casual-seeming enquiry: the more innocent the boy is, the less he understands the rules of the adult world, the more he will give away. And to judge from his posture, the boy is as guileless as the interrogator requires: we know he will blab the truth out, betray his father to the enemy, expose his secret place.

I feel like an interrogator myself. 'When did you last see *your* father?' I want to warn people: don't underestimate filial grief, don't think because you no longer live with your parents, have had a difficult relationship with them, are grown up and perhaps a parent yourself, don't think that will make it any easier when they die. I've become a death bore. I embarrass people at dinner parties with my morbidity. I used to think the world divided between those who have children and those who don't; now I think it divides between those

who've lost a parent and those whose parents are still alive.
Once I made people tell me their labour stories. Now I want
to hear their death stories—the heart attacks, the car crashes,
the cancers, the morgues. I start to believe that there's such a
thing as a 'good' or 'easy' death, just as there is a 'good' or
'easy' birth. And I start to write to friends when their fathers
die, something I never used to do, something I feel ashamed at
not having done before.

Letters come to me, too. Nearly always they begin: 'I
know no words can help at such a time.' Words like these do
seem to help, a bit: to have acknowledged the uselessness of
words seems to guarantee that the writer understands. No one
can live inside another person's body; no one can feel another's
pain; grief, like joy, must be a state of isolation. But the letters
suggest something different, a commonality, a hug of empathy,
and this is both a solace and chastisement. Others have known
worse; how much worse for a spouse than for a son; how
much worse to die in your thirties (as a beautiful intelligent
woman I sit next to at a dinner does, of cancer, two weeks
later) than to die at seventy-five like my father.

Consolations. Beside me on the desk is a new anthology
to review, *A Book of Consolations*. There are plenty of brisk,
snap-out-of-it sorts in there, like Walter Raleigh ('sorrows are
dangerous companions . . . the treasures of weak hearts'), or
Dr Johnson, who thought sorrow 'a kind of rust of the soul'
and recommended, much as my father would have, the
healing powers of fresh air and exercise. There is plenty of
speciousness about death, too: nothing to worry about, says
Plato; a 'dreamless sleep', a migration of the soul; the ruins of
time becoming the mansions of eternity. I hate all this lying
cheeriness and evasion. I'm more consoled by the person, lost
and awkward down the phone, who says: 'Never mind.' Or
by someone who holds me and says: 'They reckon losing a

parent makes you grow up; if that's so we'd all choose to remain children for ever.' I think of Larkin in 'Aubade' seeing off the solacers, seeing off religion,

> That vast moth-eaten musical brocade
> Created to pretend we never die,
> And specious stuff that says No rational being
> Can fear a thing it will not feel, *not seeing*
> That this is what we fear—no sight, no sound,
> No touch or taste or smell, nothing to think with,
> Nothing to love or link with,
> The anaesthetic from which none come round.

Bleakness like this—vivaciously denying a life beyond life, brightly expressing dark and nothingness—is the nearest thing to comfort I can find. But even Larkin, in the end, can do no good. Stand them up against grief, and even the greatest poems, the greatest paintings, the greatest novels lose the power to console. I used to think that solace was the point of art, or part of it; now it's failed the test, it doesn't seem to have much point at all. FICTION FICTION FICTION the shelves scream in bookshops. But to invent or be artful seems indecent to me now. I can't imagine why anyone would want to imagine. The music of what happened is the only music in my head.

The cursor pulses on the screen in front of me. Some of my friends and contemporaries have written moving elegies for their fathers. Even when my father was in the best of health, I used to sit mooning and tearful over these poems as if they were for me, as if I'd written them myself. I wanted my father to hurry up and die so that I could join the club. I wrote an elegy for a friend of his, as preparation. I ran elegiac lines for him through my head. Now he's given me my opening, and the poems won't come.

Not that he'd mind much. He thought poetry all right in

its way, so long as he didn't have to read it and I didn't suppose it a proper job. He was proud of me when I began to get poems published, but he said he couldn't understand them, and to me that was the ideal arrangement. I'd begun writing to escape him, to enter a world outside his control, so why would I have wanted him to get interested in my work? Perhaps the obscurity of some of my poems was there to keep him away— just as, I now guiltily recognize, I put him off coming to the London newspaper offices I worked at and which he wanted to see ('It'd be nice to get an impression—how many people did you say you have under you? only two?'), and which he thought were regrettable but necessary steps towards the summit: a job in Leeds or Bradford ('just down the road from here—you could do it in fifty minutes') on the *Yorkshire Post*.

Only once, with the poetry, did I relent. It was 1985, and I'd won a prize, and invited him to the awards ceremony in County Hall. He turned up in his yellow-and-white Dormobile with stickers of the places he'd visited on the back window. It was loaded with wood he'd brought down from Yorkshire because my garden, he'd decided, was in need of some rustic fencing. In a big room overlooking the Thames, surrounded by poets, publishers, literary agents, people from the Arts Council, he seemed small, shrunken, at a loss, a wine glass not a pint tankard in his hand. He wanted to enjoy himself, but he had a frowny, intimidated look about him, and I waited for him to make some withering remark about the company: 'Clever lot of buggers they think they are, eh?' Ken Livingstone was supposed to present the prize, and I knew my father had heard of *him*, but at the last minute Livingstone dropped out and another GLC lefty high-up, Tony Banks, made the speech instead. Afterwards, someone asked my father what he thought of the poem I'd won the prize for, 'The Ballad of the Yorkshire Ripper', and he replied: 'The

Yorkshire Ripper? Nothing very poetic about that bugger.'
He seemed to enjoy himself after that. We were supposed to
go on to a meal somewhere, and he began trying to organize a
large party, as if it were a midnight swim at Abersoch, everyone together, no shirkers, one big happy family. A large
number of people were urged into the back of his Dormobile,
between the rustic poles. I have suppressed the memory of
who exactly he did give a lift to that night, but in my dreams
Joseph Brodsky, Martin Amis, Craig Raine, Julian Barnes,
Salman Rushdie and Dylan Thomas's daughter are driven over
Westminster Bridge while my father explains that when you're
putting up rustic fencing you must be sure to use six-inch zinc
nails not four-inch iron.

Dreams? In truth, I don't dream of him. I dream of the
vast ribcage of a bison lying on the sheet of the desert and
being picked clean by vultures. I dream of blistered skin and
crumbling parchment and a cyclone of paper bits, a lost
masterpiece blowing about the sky. But I don't dream of him.
I've seen his initials on a car number-plate: ABM 179X. His
voice was on the answering machine for a while, a long
message about bank statements, until someone left a longer
one. I heard rasping breaths from his bedroom, but they died
when I walked in. I woke once to strange sounds and strange
red light after falling asleep watching television, but it wasn't
him. I haven't the comfort of religion. I'm not like the boy in
the Yeames painting, who knows his father is only missing,
not dead. You don't expect afterlife of an atheist. And even if
my father has found an afterlife, he'll be damned if he comes
back and admits it: 'I may not be right, but I'm never wrong.'

His only afterlife is in the will he made, more than enough
to be going on with. In his last year he added a codicil, which
changed the names of his executors, which made his executors
ex-executors. We didn't know this until we opened the safe

after the funeral. Had he done it because he was ill or brain-storming? Or to set the cat among the pigeons, to manipulate us from the grave? The books here on my shelves have countless examples of similar behaviour: what the dying do to the living—Mrs Wilcox in *Howards End* bequeathing the house to Margaret Schlegel rather than her family. Everything I consume these days seems to offer some parallel. Hospitals, deathbed scenes, farcical funerals, exploding pacemakers, the art of embalming, how to cope with bereavement, the cruel C: whatever paper I read or book I open or programme I turn on is certain to be about one of them. It makes me feel unoriginal. It makes me feel I've been caught up in a *Zeitgeist* of morbidity, a sickly *fin-de-siècle* where death is the only theme ever discussed.

My father wouldn't approve of morbidity. When I hear his voice in my head appraising what I'm writing about him, he doesn't approve of that either: 'You fathead. Seventy-five bloody years, over forty of them while you were alive yourself, and all we get is me looking like death warmed up. You daft sod—do you think that dying is anything to write home about, that it's any sort of story? Let's hear about some of the good times, the holidays, the golf and tennis. What's the big deal about death? No, tell them how good with my hands I could be, all the fun we had and things we built, how I loved you and Gill and Mummy, how I tried to leave the world a better place. And leave Auntie Beaty out of it: it was a phase, no more. There are people who have to be protected here. What else is there to say?'

Yes, Dad, I know I should leave Beaty out, but she is part of your story, and of mine. 'Auntie' Beaty, rather: you always called her that, as if the name could give her status as one of the family, as a relation or godparent, *one of us*, or perhaps because it seemed natural to a man who called his wife 'Mummy' to call the other woman he loved 'Auntie'.

Now that you're gone she has taken to ringing me. Fluttery, giddy, birdlike, she tells me how like you I sound. If she could see me as I stand there trying to make sense of this—in your shoes, your socks, your jumper, your blazer— she'd say I *looked* like you, too. For years I've sat among your hand-me-down furniture, lived off your money, driven your two-year-old cars (each time you bought a new one, you'd trade in mine and let me have your better one for nothing). Now there's something more—your face staring back each time I look in the mirror. 'Oh, you're *just* like him,' Beaty says. Maybe I *am* you.

She rings Mum, too—and has been to see her. Odd to think that one of the first people to stay with my mother— after the relations from Ireland, after Auntie Hilly, after Kela —should be Beaty, who once caused her such pain. Odder, even, than thinking that Beaty would want to go and comfort the woman who kept you from her for more than a few hours a week. I can see they have something in common, but this common ground must also be a great source of pain. What have they to talk about but you? And what could be harder for them to talk about than you? I used to think they were friends only for appearance's sake, because you gave them no choice. Now it's what they choose. And Beaty, no doubt of it, is good for my mother—cheers her up, takes her out of herself, makes her feel better. Beaty is her friend.

A few days after she's left my mother, Beaty sends me a letter—photographs and chit-chat mainly, but with a sealed envelope as well, marked BLAKE: PERSONAL. I think this inner letter must be the confession I've been waiting for, the key to everything, but when I open it I find not revelations but Revelations—a rush of spiritual fragments and poetry: 'Without him, the world is going to feel empty, like a shell—I must be in heaven'; 'As I glanced back at the coffin my soul cried out in pain: how could we leave you there?' 'I loved you so, but as the family did.'

I pore over the last words and write back the next day, in a sealed envelope, the same protective device. I tell her I know something of your relationship. I invite her to tell me more—I don't mind what she tells me, I say, so long as she feels able to grieve for you like the rest of us. I write that it was all a long time ago, that time is a great healer, that I'm an adult now, whom she can address as an adult. I realize there's something calculating in these kind, forgiving words, that they're there in part to draw her out, to snare her like a robin in the snow. I know that I'm angry with her on some level, too, or had been angry once—angry on my own behalf, resentful of the secrets you pretended weren't there but which I sensed *were* there, and were important; angry on my mother's behalf, with her suddenly-packed suitcase at the bottom of the stairs. With a letter, though, that anger might be allayed. A few days later it comes:

> Dear Blake,
> Arthur always said never to put anything in writing. But hopefully here are some pieces in your jigsaw.
>
> Your mother asked me the afternoon I got there. I was sitting on the stool in the kitchen, frozen from the train and hugging the Aga. 'You two had a long affair, didn't you?' I think I'd rather she'd hit me, not stay so calm.
>
> You know, Blake, Arthur was always the patron saint of lost causes—in his compassion he could see mine was a sad marriage. I was so alone. It was only because of him I could laugh—now I don't know how to get through the day. I have lost my mentor, and so have you.

I know he loved your mother more than anybody
on earth. He loved Gill and you so very much. He
was proud of and loved you all.

Please leave me one last small piece—it's mine.

Whatever sadness I am sorry for.

Your loving Beaty

'Please leave me one last small piece. It's mine.' Simple,
obvious, unanswerable—why hadn't I anticipated it? People
had told me I was arrogant, prying into my father's private
business, thinking I had some right of access. But I thought
since I was forgiving Beaty I was entitled to some knowledge
in return. I convinced myself that without that knowledge I
could never make sense of my childhood or of my present—
my work, my marriage, or the bits of them that seemed to be
connected with being my father's son. Perhaps I even thought
that if she told me everything I'd get him back—that he
wouldn't be dead. Now I know that's wrong. I'd been
behaving as my father used to when he walked straight into
patients' homes without knocking. Now I see the doors are
locked. Now I know I'll never know the truth about him and
Beaty. Even if I did, it couldn't matter. My father's affair is his
affair. His story is not my story. And Beaty doesn't have the
missing piece. There is no missing piece, only grief.

I tell the therapist this, as if it were a great discovery. Yes,
Dad, a therapist. I know you don't approve, I know you're
pretty down on analysts, male or female (and this one's
female), and yes *of course* I should have shopped around and
found a cheaper one, or at least should have asked this one,
instead of supinely writing the cheque: 'How much for cash?'
But I do have to talk to someone; I'm not going to get
through this alone. Not that we hit it off together all that well,
she and I. There is no couch in her room, though there are

beanbags, and a baseball bat to hit them with. Myself, I don't use the baseball bat, nor scream, nor weep. I sit in a white canvas chair, the sort film directors have, and I play her back bits of my life. She catches me smiling at critical points of my psycho-story, and this, she says, or gets me to say, is because I'm trying to distance myself ironically from my emotions. She tells me I'm a poor communicator, that I don't listen to what my body's telling me, that I give out ambivalent signals. All of this is true, and helpful—so helpful that soon, I think, I shall stop seeing her.

In July I go up to Yorkshire—the first time in seven months. The village wants to remember you, Dad. You were going to be a bench at first, but there is a bench already, for someone else. Then you were going to be a tree, but they worried that in digging the hole they'd sever gas pipes or electric cables. So you have become a sundial instead— watching for the sun (as you always did), sleeping out over-night, plenty of fresh air. Under the trees we planted at the front of the old house, the trees that for years wouldn't grow in the clay but are tall now, under those trees, out by the road, they erect a sundial. Back at the house, the wind blows through the delphiniums and the roses not yet deadheaded. The rustic fencing you put up rots at its own feet. The raspberries have mildew—they're grey and ashy like a dead mouse, and dissolve in the wind.

The ashes themselves, your ashes, have been kept in a big sheeny-brown plastic jar at the bottom of the wardrobe, and we've chosen today to scatter them. I take the jar down the garden, unscrew the lid, dip my hand in and taste a few grey specks: a smoky nothingness on my tongue. You, or your coffin, or a crematorium pick 'n' mix, how can I tell? My mother and sister come, and we start to pour helpings of you among your favourite bits of the garden. We take it in turns, filling the lid of the jar with fine shale (like those upturned lids we used to fill with mouse poison and leave behind the fridge), then tossing the shale to the wind. The wind blows powder back in our faces; a speck catches in my sister's eye, her good eye; my trouser bottoms are sifted in volcanic dust. You cover the flower-bed like fine spray, every leaf variegated. We keep on scattering till the jar is tipped up for the last time. My mother hugs my sister. I walk off with the jar, which is like a giant pill-box, and hear your voice in the wind: 'Useful container that—I should hang on to it.' I stow it in the garage between the jump leads and a shrunken plastic bottle of anti-freeze.

In London again, at Greenwich District, I check my heart out. 'Always listen to your own heart,' didn't you say, and I have been, to those extra-systoles and odd hollowings-out and things that go bump in the night. 'A bit slow if anything,' says the cardiologist as I lie there, a row of milking-teats wired to my chest. I leave feeling like a hypochondriac, afraid of becoming the kind of patient you always hated, who'd turn up at the house—*at the house*, not surgery—unannounced.

In August I go back to Yorkshire. Eight months on and you're still in the headlines. SUNDIAL MEMORIAL STOLEN AFTER TWO DAYS, the paper says: 'A plaque to local doctor Arthur Morrison, cemented in place on Friday, was vandalized and removed by Sunday.' The parish council has had a re-think: you are going to be a bench after all. I sit with my mother outside the study, two recliners and two teas in the wind, and her words stream over me—an undammed beck, the release and relief of talking to someone. The hay has turned from green to brass, and the wind passes through it like a flu-shiver. It's more beautiful than I've ever seen it—even after the tractor has been, cutting the field in an hour, the rows of hay like bodies after a plane crash waiting to be identified. 'How's

215

your saga coming along?' she asks, meaning these words I've been writing about you. I show her a bit. 'It's good about Dad,' she says. 'True to life. But this stuff about Beaty and Sandra . . . ' We sit on, inhaling the new-mownness, not wanting to give up, not wanting to let go.

Back in London, the therapist asks: 'How long did you say it had been now?'

'How long has what been?'

'Since the death. When did you last see your father?'

I remember the answer then. I tell her.

He isn't drinking, isn't eating. He wears his trousers open at the waist, held up not by a belt but by pain and swelling. He looks like death, but he is not dead, and won't be for another four weeks. He has driven down from Yorkshire to London. He has made it against the odds. He is still my father. He is still here.

'I've brought some plants for you.'

'Come and sit down first, Dad, you've been driving for hours.'

'No, best get them unloaded.'

It's like Birnam Wood coming to Dunsinane, black plastic bags and wooden boxes blooming in the back seat, the rear window, the boot: herbs, hypericum, escallonia, cotoneaster, ivies, potentillas. He directs me where to leave the different plants—which will need shade, which sun, which shelter. Like all my father's presents, they come with a pay-off—he will not leave until he has seen every one of them planted: 'I know you. And I don't want them drying up.'

We walk round the house, the expanse of rooms, so different from the old flat. 'It's wonderful to see you settled at last,' he says, and I resist telling him that I'm not settled, have never felt less settled in my life. I see his eyes taking in the little things to be done, the leaky taps, the cracked paint, the rotting window-frames.

'You'll need a new switch unit for the mirror light—the contact has gone, see.'

'Yes.'

'And a couple of two-inch Phillips screws will solve this.'

'I've got some. Let's have a drink now, eh.'

'What's the schedule for tomorrow?' he asks, as always, and I'm irritated, as always, at his need to parcel out the weekend into a series of tasks, as if without a plan of action it wouldn't be worth his coming, not even to see his son or grandchildren. 'I don't think I'll be much help to you,' he says, 'but I'll try.' By nine-thirty he is in bed and asleep.

I wake him next day at nine, unthinkably late, with a pint-mug of tea, unthinkably refused. After his breakfast of strawberry Complan he comes round the house with me, stooped and crouching over his swollen stomach. For once it's me who is going to have to do the hammering and screwing. We go down to the hardware shop in Greenwich, where he charms the socks off the black assistant, who gives me a shrug and pat at the end, as if to say, 'Where d'you get a Dad like this from?' Back home again, he decides that the job for him is to get the curtains moving freely on their rails. 'You know the best thing for it?' he says. 'Furniture polish. Get me a can of it and I'll sort it for you.' He teeters on a wooden kitchen stool at each of the windows in the house, his trousers gaping open, and sprays polish on the rail, and wipes it over with a dirty rag. His balance looks precarious. I try to talk him down, but he is stubborn.

'No, it needs doing. And every time you pull the curtains from now on, you can think of me.'

I ask him about the operation: is he apprehensive?

217

'No point in being. They have to have a look. I expect it's an infarct, and they'll be able to cure that, but if not . . . well, I've had a good life and I've left everything in order for you.'

'I'd rather you than order.'

'Too true.'

I make sure there are only two light but time-consuming jobs for us. The first is to fix a curtain pole across the garden end of the kitchen, over the glazed door, and we spend the best part of two hours bickering about the best way to do this: there's a problem on the left-hand side because the kitchen cupboards finish close to the end wall, six inches or so, and you can't get an electric drill in easily to make the holes for the fixing bracket. The drill keeps sheering off, partly because I'm unnerved by him below, drawing something on the back of an envelope. I get down and he shows me his plan: a specially mounted shelf in the side wall to support the pole rather than a fixing bracket for it on the end. Sighing and cursing, I climb back up and follow his instructions in every detail—not just the size of screws and Rawlplugs needed, but how to clasp the hammer:

'Hold it at the end, you daft sod, not up near the top.'

'Christ, Dad, I'm forty-one years old.'

'And you still don't know how to hold a hammer properly —or a screwdriver.'

Infuriatingly, his plan works—the shelf mounting, the pole, the curtain, all fine. I try not to give him the satisfaction of admitting it.

We bicker our way into the next room and the other job: to hang the chandelier inherited from Uncle Bert. At some point in the move, many of the glass pieces have become separated, and now, in the dim November light behind the tall sash-window, we spend the afternoon working out where they belong, reattaching them to the wire that joins them, and then strengthening the candelabra from which they dangle. 'This really needs soldering,' he says, meaning that he will find an alternative to soldering them, since to solder would mean going out and spending money on a soldering iron when he has a perfectly good one at home. I watch him bowed over the glass diamonds, with pliers and fractured screw-threads and nuts and bits of wire—the improviser, the amateur inventor—and I think of all the jobs he's done for me down the years, and how sooner or later I'll have to learn to do them for myself. The metal clasps joining glass ball to glass ball are like the clasps on his King Edward cigar boxes, and the clasps on his student skeleton, Janet.

'I think that's it,' he says, attaching a last bauble. 'Three pieces missing, but no one will notice.' He stands at the foot of the stepladder holding the heavy chandelier while I connect the two electrical wires to the ceiling rose, tighten the rose-cover and slip the ring-attachment over the dangling hook. He lets go tentatively—'Gently does it'—unable to believe, since he has not done the fixing himself, that the chandelier will hold. It holds. We turn the light on, and the six candle-bulbs shimmer through the cage of glass, the prison of prisms. 'Let there be light,' my father says, the only time I can ever remember him quoting anything, though I can recall some joke he used to tell, about failed floodlights at Turf Moor, a visiting Chinese football team, and the punch-line 'Many hands make light work'. We stand there gawping upwards for a moment, as if we had witnessed a miracle, or as if this were a grand ballroom, not a suburban dining-room, and the next dance, if we had the courage to take part in it, might be the beginning of a new life. Then he turns the switch off and it's dark again and he says: 'Excellent. What's the next job, then?'

For further information about Granta Books
and a full list of titles, please write to us at

Granta Books

2/3 HANOVER YARD

NOEL ROAD

LONDON

N1 8BE

enclosing a stamped, addressed envelope

———————————

You can visit our website at

http://www.granta.com